Assessing the

Human-Animal Bond

New Directions in the Human-Animal Bond
Alan M. Beck, series editor

Assessing the
Human-Animal Bond

A Compendium of
Actual Measures

compiled by David C. Anderson

Purdue University Press
West Lafayette, Indiana

Printed in the United States of America.

ISBN 978-1-55753-424-8
      1-55753-424-1

Library of Congress Cataloging-in-Publication Data

Assessing the human-animal bond : a compendium of actual measures / [edited by] David C. Anderson.
      p. cm. — (New directions in the human-animal bond)
  Reprints of works originally published from 1985–2003.
  Includes bibliographical references (p.   ) and index.
  ISBN-13: 978-1-55753-424-8 (alk. paper) 1. Pets—Social aspects—Measurement. 2. Human-animal
relationships—Measurement. 3. Surveys. I. Anderson, David Charles, 1931–
  SF411.5.A87 2006
  636.088'7—dc22

                                                                                2006027748

Contents

Foreword

Within the last 30 years the study of the impact of companion animals on people has evolved from a hobby of pet owners to an appreciation of the human-animal bond as a recognized concept. The "bond" is now even an area worthy of scientific study at institutions of higher learning all over the world. The "bond" is a topic of study in a variety of academic disciplines, including psychology, nursing, geriatrics, child development, social work, and animal behavior. There is ever developing evidence that the bond between people and their companion animals contributes to improving human health.

From the very beginning researchers have struggled with how to assess the nature of the bond, for without that understanding, appreciation of the complexity of the interaction would not be possible. Over the years scholars from a variety of disciplines have developed and validated a number of measures to assess the bond. Many researchers spend much time tracking down the published measures they may use as they plan their own studies. David Anderson has put the major recognized instruments to assess the human-animal bond all in one place. As important, he has included the appropriate citations and notes on validation of each instrument, which is required for the serious researcher.

All researchers who are interested in studying the human-animal bond will find this book one of the most used books in their library. It is the resource book that everyone said was needed, and now is available.

Dr. Alan M. Beck
School of Veterinary Medicine
Purdue University

Introduction

Assessing the Human-Animal Bond: A Compendium of Actual Measures gathers in one place those measures presently used to study the human-companion animal bond. In addition, it attempts to list related measures (e.g., guided interviews and picture tests) and direct readers to their sources. It deals only with those measures which relate to humans and their companion animals, principally by attachment or bonding, but also by fear, abuse and neglect.

Assessing the Human-Animal Bond does not attempt to include attitude scales. Daniel Kossow, while a graduate student at the Tufts Center for Animals and Public Policy, compiled a bibliography of surveys on public attitudes towards animals and animal-related issues.[1] In 2000 Harold Herzog and Lorna Dorr published an article on electronically available surveys of attitudes towards animals.[2] It has been estimated that 40 percent of the human-animal studies literature focuses on human attitudes toward animals.

The measures chosen for inclusion are those most heavily used by researchers, as well as measures that appear to be innovative or relate to different aspects of the companion animal-human relationship. Unfortunately, some of those were not available.

Each section is devoted to a single measure and begins with its name and citation. In the most complex situations, the section first cites the work in which the scale is first used, followed by citations to works in which the measure is validated or further developed and citations to works in which the measure is used. Relevant notes are then listed and a copyright notice appears on the page before the scale. Many of the scales are slightly modified: British and Canadian spellings have been americanized; and introductory remarks for the client, instructions for returning the measure, and thanks have largely been eliminated. With the exception of the Melson Pet Attachment Scale—Revised, the measure itself completes the section in reproducible sheets. The full Melson PAS requires 240 pages, but instructions given here should provide sufficient information for researchers to complete the scale.

Both the International Society for AnthroZoology and the Animals & Society Institute plan for their respective journals, *Anthrozoös* and *Society & Animals,* to be readily available on the Internet. Where applicable, reference is made to a specific website for an article or an individual measure published in their journals.

Typically, North American research presents the measure used, while European research does not. Whether the measure is presented in the article or not, the exact questions and the way in which the measure is handled may often be deduced from a close reading. For example, the 1985 Kidd & Kidd article on children's attitudes about pets uses an open-ended interview with 300 children.[3] The interview questions are not separately stated, but by reading the methodology and results sections, one can reconstruct the interview questions. To aid researchers to that end, a list of Aline and Robert Kidd's articles on the human-companion animal relationship is included as an appendix.

The Index and Annotated Bibliography of Related Scales lists the scales presented in the main section of this book and presents details on related measures. A name index to this index/bibliography is included.

The author's thanks and deep appreciation go to the authors and publishers of these measures and their willingness to permit their publication or reprinting here.

---

1. Attitudes towards animals and animal issues: A historical perspective in the US. www.tufts.edu/vet/cfa/surveys.html (accessed January 28, 2005).
2. Herzog, Harold A.; Dorr, Lorna B. Electronically available surveys of attitudes toward animals. *Society & Animals,* 9(2) 2000:183–90 www.psyeta.org/sa/sa8.2/herzog.shtml (accessed August 20, 2005).
3. Kidd, A. H.; Kidd, R. M. Children's attitudes about pets. *Psychological Reports,* 57(1) 1985 Aug:15–31. In recognition of the authors' thoroughness in presenting the results of the unpublished interview questionnaire, the database Health and Psychosocial Instruments assigned the questionnaire used in this research the title Children and Pets (C & P).

CENSHARE Pet Attachment Scale, PAS

(Holcomb, Williams & Richards, 1985),
also known as Pet Attachment Scale, PAS

Described and validated in:

Daly, Kathy. Case control study of anorexia nervosa and pet ownership and attachment. 1985. 137 leaves: illus. Unpublished M.P.H. (Plan B) thesis, University of Minnesota, 1985. Seen in part.

> The earliest version of the CENSHARE PAS appears as "Attachment questionnaire A," leaves 128-30. Twenty-nine items are used, all in the past tense. The first item, "Your pet bit, growled or hissed at you," and the fifth item, "You verbally or physically disciplined your pet when she/he failed to obey or did something inappropriate," have been dropped from the current 27-item, validated CENSHARE PAS.

Holcomb, Ralph; Williams, R. Craig; Richards, P. Scott. The elements of attachment: Relationship maintenance and intimacy. *Journal of the Delta Society,* 2(1) 1985 Winter:28–34.

> Table 2: "The CENSHARE Pet Attachment Survey," a 27-item self report, Scale 1, Relationship Maintenance, and Scale 2, Intimacy (page 31).

Used in:

Budge, R. Claire; Spicer, John; Jones, Boyd; St. George, Ross. Health correlates of compatibility and attachment in human-companion animal relationships. *Society & Animals,* 6(3) 1998:219–34.

> Use the Animal Human Compatibility Scale (Budge, Jones, Spicer, 1997), the [CENSHARE] PAS, the Interpersonal Support Evaluation List, ISEL (Cohen et al., 1985), Mental Health Inventory, MHI (Veit, Ware, 1983), and the Inventory of Limbic Languidness (Pennebaker, 1982).

Gosse, Gerald H.; Barnes, Michael J. Human grief resulting from the death of a pet. *Anthrozoös,* 7(2) 1994:103–12.

> Use the Grief Experience Inventory, CENSHARE PAS Intimacy scale revised into the past tense, the Schedule of Recent Experience, and a Questionnaire for Pet Owners.

Jarolmen, Joann. A comparison of the grief reaction of children and adults: Focusing on pet loss and bereavement. *Omega,* 37(2) 1998:133–50.

> Uses the CENSHARE PAS Intimacy scale revised into the past tense by Gosse and Barnes, the Grief Experience Inventory, and "Questions for Each Person in the Study." The last is given in Table 1, page 137.

Johnson, Suzanne B.; Rule, Warren R. Personality characteristics and self-esteem in pet owners and nonowners. *International Journal of Psychology,* 26(2) 1991:241–52.

> Use the CENSHARE PAS, the Self-Esteem Scale, Texas Social Behavior Inventory (10-item inventory), Eysenck Personality Inventory, and a short version of the Social Desirability Scale.

Marks, Shaela G.; Koepke, Jean E.; Bradley, Cheryl L. Pet attachment and generativity among young adults. *Journal of Psychology,* 128(6) 1994 Nov:641–50.

Use the CENSHARE PAS, the Pet Attitude Inventory (Wilson, Netting, New, 1987) and the Loyola Generativity Scale (LGS) (McAdams and de St. Aubin, 1992).

Notarangelo, Kathy Elizabeth. Personality characteristics of dog owners with specific breed preferences. 1999. xii, 104 leaves. Unpublished Ph.D. thesis, California School of Professional Psychology, Berkeley-Alameda, 1999. Not seen. Abstract in *Dissertation Abstracts International,* Section B: The Sciences & Engineering, 61(1-B) 2000 Jul:576-B.

Uses an experimenter-designed questionnaire to measure demographics and life characteristics, the Adjective Check List (ACL) to determine personality self-description, and the CENSHARE PAS.

Planchon, Lynn A.; Templer, Donald I.; Stokes, Shelley; Keller, Jacqueline. Death of a companion cat or dog and human bereavement: Psychosocial variables. *Society & Animals,* 10(1) 2002:93–105.

Use the Beck Depression Inventory, the CENSHARE PAS, the Death Depression Scale (Beck et al., 1961), the Pet Attitude Scale (Templer et al., 1981), and the Pet Loss Questionnaire.

This article is available at the Animals & Society Institute website, www.societyandanimalsforum.org.

Stevens, Linda T. Attachment to pets among eighth graders. *Anthrozoös,* 3(3) 1990:177–82.

Notes:

Reverse score items 2, 13, 19, and 20.

The version distributed by CENSHARE includes the statement "Prepared by Ralph Holcomb, PhD."

The CENSHARE Pet Attachment Survey is also available from the Behavioral Measurement Database Services, BMDS, producer of the Health and Psychosocial Instruments (HaPI) database. Phone 412/687-6850, fax 412/687-5213, or email bmdshapi@aol.com for ordering information. Supply the HaPI accession number 52474 and the title, CENSHARE Pet Attachment Survey.

Copyright Notice:

CENSHARE Pet Attachment Survey

		Almost Always	Often	Sometimes	Almost Never
1.	Within your family, your pet likes you best.	1	2	3	4
2.	You are too busy to spend time with your pet.	1	2	3	4
3.	You spend time each day playing with or exercising your pet.	1	2	3	4
4.	Your pet comes to greet you when you arrive.	1	2	3	4
5.	You talk to your pet as a friend.	1	2	3	4
6.	Your pet is aware of your different moods.	1	2	3	4
7.	Your pet pays attention and obeys you quickly.	1	2	3	4
8.	You confide in your pet.	1	2	3	4
9.	You play with your pet when he/she approaches.	1	2	3	4
10.	You spend time each day training your pet.	1	2	3	4
11.	You show photos of your pet to your friends.	1	2	3	4
12.	You spend time each day grooming your pet.	1	2	3	4
13.	You ignore your pet when he/she approaches.	1	2	3	4
14.	When you come home, your pet is the first one you greet.	1	2	3	4
15.	Your pet tries to stay near by following you.	1	2	3	4

	Almost Always	Often	Sometimes	Almost Never
16. You buy presents for your pet.	1	2	3	4
17. When you feel bad, you seek your pet for comfort.	1	2	3	4
18. You prefer to be with your pet more than with most people you know.	1	2	3	4
19. When your pet misbehaves, you hit him/her.	1	2	3	4
20. Your pet is a nuisance and a bother to you.	1	2	3	4
21. You consider your pet to be a member of your family.	1	2	3	4
22. You like to touch and stroke your pet.	1	2	3	4
23. You feel sad when you are separated from your pet.	1	2	3	4
24. You like to have your pet sleep near your bed.	1	2	3	4
25. You like to have your pet sleep on your bed.	1	2	3	4
26. You have your pet near you when you study, read, or watch TV.	1	2	3	4
27. You don't like your pet to get too close to you.	1	2	3	4

Center for the Study of Animal Wellness
Pet Bonding Scale, CSAWPBS
(Johnson, Meadows, 2003)

This 28-item measure is based on a review of extant literature and on the authors' preliminary studies. It is designed to elicit participants' responses to receiving dog visits in a therapeutic context. The CSAWPBS is designed to measure the concepts of unconditional acceptance from the animal, feelings of reciprocity in the visit, and feelings of attachment to the animal. The measure takes approximately 10 minutes to administer. It has been found to be internally consistent with a coefficient alpha level of 0.892 among 15 disabled adult public housing residents ranging in age from 40 to 85, who participated in a graduated walking program with trained visitor dogs.

Evaluated in:

Fulton, Barbie. Evaluation of the reliability of the Center for the Study of Animal Wellness Pet Bonding Scale (CSAWPBS) and the Dog Walk Program. 2005. 38 leaves; illus. Unpublished research project, University of Missouri-Columbia, 2005.

Notes:

The original document was written within a grid in which the participants marked an X in the appropriate square to describe their views.

Copyright Notice:

Center for the Study of Animal Wellness (CSAW) Pet Bonding Scale

Below are some statements about people's views about their visits with dog visitors. Please mark the number after each statement that best describes your views.

	More often true				More often false
1. The dog visitor likes me.	1	2	3	4	5
2. I talk to the dog visitor.	1	2	3	4	5
3. I confide in the dog visitor.	1	2	3	4	5
4. The dog visitor understands what I say.	1	2	3	4	5
5. The dog visitor knows when I feel bad.	1	2	3	4	5
6. The dog visitor is always glad to see me.	1	2	3	4	5
7. The dog visitor prefers me to others.	1	2	3	4	5
8. The dog visitor has become my friend.	1	2	3	4	5
9. I look forward to getting up in the morning on days when I will see the dog visitor.	1	2	3	4	5
10. I tell others about the dog visitor.	1	2	3	4	5
11. The dog visitor knows when I feel happy	1	2	3	4	5
12. I would like to have the dog visitor come to my home.	1	2	3	4	5
13. I will remember the dog visitor after my program.	1	2	3	4	5
14. The dog visitor makes walking easier.	1	2	3	4	5
	More often true				More often false

		More often true				More often false
15. The dog visitor tries to comfort me.		1	2	3	4	5
16. The dog visits make me feel better.		1	2	3	4	5
17. The dog visits are boring.		1	2	3	4	5
18. I feel attached to the dog visitor.		1	2	3	4	5
19. The dog visits give me energy.		1	2	3	4	5
20. I miss the dog visitor between visits.		1	2	3	4	5
21. The dog doesn't judge me.		1	2	3	4	5
22. I look forward to the dog visits.		1	2	3	4	5
23. The dog visits make me feel happy.		1	2	3	4	5
24. The dog accepts me just the way I am.		1	2	3	4	5
25. I make the dog feel better.		1	2	3	4	5
26. I make the dog feel happy.		1	2	3	4	5
27. The dog takes my mind off my troubles.		1	2	3	4	5
28. The dog helps me feel secure.		1	2	3	4	5
		More often true				More often false

Childhood Pet Ownership Questionnaire
(Paul, Serpell, 1993)

Developed for:

Paul, E. S.; Serpell, J. A. Childhood pet keeping and humane attitudes in young adulthood. *Animal Welfare,* 2(4) 1993 Nov:321–37.

The Childhood Pet Ownership Questionnaire is not reproduced in this article.

Use the Pet Attitude Scale (Templer et al., 1981), a modified, updated and anglicized version of the Scale of Attitudes towards the Treatment of Animals (Bowd, 1984), the Empathy Scale (Mehrabian & Epstein, 1972), and a Charity donations test. Some of these are not reproduced here. The Charity Donations Test has been americanized.

Reported in:

Paul, Elizabeth; Serpell, James. Pets and the development of positive attitudes to animals, pages 127–44, in: Manning, Aubrey; Serpell, James (editors). *Animals and human society: Changing perspectives.* London; New York: Routledge, 1994.

Childhood Pet Ownership Questionnaire

This questionnaire has been designed to find out about your experiences with pet animals during your childhood, about the pets that you own now or might like to own in the future, and about your attitudes towards yourself, other people, animals and the natural environment. There are no right or wrong answers. Please answer all the questions by checking the appropriate boxes and by filling in specific details on the lines provided. The whole questionnaire should take about 20 minutes to complete.

1. Age: _____ years

2. Sex: Female _____ Male _____

3. Nationality: _____

4. Qualification being studied for: B.A. _____ B.S. _____ Ph.D. _____ Other _____

5. Year of course/research project: 1st _____ 2nd _____ 3rd _____ Other _____

6. Subject of study/research: _____

7. (Graduate students only): Subject of first degree: _____

SECTION 1: Your Childhood

Note: In this questionnaire, "childhood" refers to the period up to and including 16 years of age.

1. Father's occupation (during your childhood) _____

2. Mother's occupation (during your childhood) _____

3. During your childhood was your mother mostly:

    At home   _____

    Working part-time outside the home   _____

    Working full-time outside the home   _____

4. How many brothers and sisters did you have? _____

5. Were you:

    An only child   _____

    The oldest child in the family   _____

    The youngest child in the family   _____

    A middle child (i.e., with older and younger siblings)   _____

6. Was your childhood home (or the home you lived in for the longest part of your childhood) situated in a:

High rise development	_____
Built-up area with no open space nearby	_____
Built-up area with nearby open space or large garden	_____
Country district	_____

7. Please give details of the number (or approximate number) of pets you and your family kept during your childhood (up to and including 16 years of age). Do not include the offspring of existing pets that were only kept for a short while (e.g., litters of kittens, puppies, etc.).

Type of pet	Number owned by you (kept by you specifically)	Number kept by other members of your family or by the family as a whole
Horses, ponies or donkeys	_____	_____
Dogs	_____	_____
Cats	_____	_____
Small mammals (e.g., rabbit, mouse, hamster, guinea pig)	_____	_____
Birds	_____	_____
Fish, reptiles, amphibians, insects, spiders, etc.	_____	_____
Others. Please specify:		
_____	_____	_____
_____	_____	_____

8. During your childhood, did you or your family have any pets that you would say were important to you?

Yes___ No___

If **no,** please go on to question 9. If **yes,** please give details below of all the pets that were important to you. List these pets in order of importance to you, the most important first.

Type of pet (i.e., cat, dog, mouse, etc.)	Your age range (approx.) when you had this pet.	Was this pet (1) fairly important, 2) very important, or (3) extremely important to you?
_____	_____years to _____years	(1)___ (2)___ (3)___
_____	_____years to _____years	(1)___ (2)___ (3)___
_____	_____years to _____years	(1)___ (2)___ (3)___
_____	_____years to _____years	(1)___ (2)___ (3)___

9. As a child, do you remember ever really wanting to have or longing for a particular type of pet?

      Yes___   No___

If **no,** please go on to question 10. If **yes,** please give details below, of any types of pets that you really wanted at some time during your childhood (up to and including 16 years of age).

Type of Pet	Do you remember ever really wanting to have this type of pet?		About how old were you then?	How strongly did you want this type of pet? (1) Fairly, (2) Very, or (3) Extremely strongly.	Did you ever get a pet of this type?	
Horses, ponies, or donkeys	Yes ___	No ___	___ years	(1)__ (2)__ (3)__	Yes ___	No ___
Dogs	Yes ___	No ___	___ years	(1)__ (2)__ (3)__	Yes ___	No ___
Cats	Yes ___	No ___	___ years	(1)__ (2)__ (3)__	Yes ___	No ___
Small mammals e.g., rabbit, mouse, etc.	Yes ___	No ___	___ years	(1)__ (2)__ (3)__	Yes ___	No ___
Birds	Yes ___	No ___	___ years	(1)__ (2)__ (3)__	Yes ___	No ___
Fish, reptiles, amphibians, insects, spiders, etc.	Yes ___	No ___	___ years	(1)__ (2)__ (3)__	Yes ___	No ___
Others (please specify) _____	Yes ___	No ___	___ years	(1)__ (2)__ (3)__	Yes ___	No ___
_____	Yes ___	No ___	___ years	(1)__ (2)__ (3)__	Yes ___	No ___

10. In general, were your mother's attitudes to pets:

    Extremely positive   ___

    Very positive   ___

    Fairly positive   ___

    Neither positive nor negative   ___

    Negative   ___

11. In general, were your father's attitudes to pets:

    Extremely positive   ___

    Very positive   ___

    Fairly positive   ___

    Neither positive nor negative   ___

    Negative   ___

SECTION 2: Pets and Other Animals

1. Do you have any pets at the moment?

    Yes ___   No___

    If **yes,** what are they? _____

    _____

2. Would you like to own any pets in the future, if and when your circumstances allow it?

    Yes ___   No ___

    If **yes,** what would those pets be? Please list them in order of their importance to you, the one you would most like to own coming first. You may list as many or as few as you like.

    1st_____   2nd_____   3rd_____

    4th_____   5th_____   6th_____

3. Do you regularly take part in any of the following hobbies or activities?

    Bird watching   Yes___   No___

    Fishing   Yes___   No___

    Horse riding   Yes___   No___

    Hunting animals (of any sort)   Yes___   No___

4. Do you belong to any organizations or charities involved in or concerned with improving the welfare of animals?

    Yes___   No___

5. Do you belong to any organizations or charities involved in or concerned with conservation of the natural environment?

    Yes___   No___

6. Are there any foods that you do not eat for ethical or moral (but not religious reasons) reasons?

    Yes___   No___

    If **yes**:   (a) What types of food do you avoid eating? _____

               (b) About how old were you when you started to avoid eating these foods? _____ years

7. While you were at school, did you do any experiments, as part of your studies, that involved any invasive or medical procedures being carried out on living animals, or the use of dead animals (for dissections, etc.)?

    Yes___   No___   If **yes,** what species were used: _____

8. During your undergraduate course, have you done/did you do any experiments, as part of your studies, that involved any invasive or medical procedures being carried out on living animals, or the use of dead animals (for dissections, etc.)?

    Yes___   No___   If **yes,** what species were used: _____

9. (Graduate students only): During your postgraduate course/research, have you done/are you doing any experiments, as part of your studies, that involve any invasive or medical procedures being carried out on living animals, or the use of dead animals (for dissections, etc.)?

    Yes___   No___   If **yes,** what species were used: _____

SECTION 3: Children and Pets

1. Do you think that any of the pets you or your family had when you were a child had any positive effects on you (i.e., were good for you in any way)?

    Yes___   No___   Had no pets___

    If **yes,** in what ways do you think they were good for you?

    _____

    _____

    _____

2. Do you think that any of the pets you or your family had when you were a child had any negative effects on you (i.e., were bad for you in any way)?

    Yes___   No___   Had no pets___

    If **yes,** in what ways do you think they were bad for you?

    _____

    _____

    _____

3. Do you have any children?

    Yes___   No___   If **yes,** how many?_____

4. In the future, how many children do you think you would like to have (in total)?

    None___   1 or 2___   3 or 4___   5 or more___

SECTION 4: Attitude Scales

This section, of four attitude measures, is omitted from this book. The first measure is the Empathy Scale (Mehrabian & Epstein, 1972) lacking the two pet animal empathy questions. The third measure is the Pet Attitude Scale (Templer et al., 1981). The fourth measure is a modified, updated, and anglicized version of the Scale of Attitudes towards the Treatment of Animals (Bowd, 1984). These three scales use a nine-point Likert scale (Agree very strongly, 4—3—2—1—0—1—2—3—4, Disagree very strongly). The second measure reads as follows:

Scale 2

Please show how often you feel the way described in each of the following statements by drawing a circle around the appropriate number for each one.

	Never	Rarely	Sometimes	Often
1. I lack companionship.	1	2	3	4
2. There is no one I can turn to.	1	2	3	4
3. I am an outgoing person.	1	2	3	4
	Never	Rarely	Sometimes	Often
4. I feel left out.	1	2	3	4
5. I feel isolated from others.	1	2	3	4
6. I can find companionship when I want it.	1	2	3	4
7. I am unhappy being so withdrawn.	1	2	3	4
8. People are around me but not with me.	1	2	3	4

SECTION 5: Charities

Imagine that you have $US 500 to donate to charity. Please indicate how much of this money you would give to each of the following (fictional) charities. You can give all the money to one charity, or spread it across as many as you like. You must donate all of the money. Do not divide the money into sums smaller than $US 5.

1. This charity works to protect important wildlife habitats, especially those which are vitally important for the preservation of rare plants and birds.

    $_____

2. This charity raises money for research to be undertaken into the prevention and cure of all forms of cancer.

    $_____

3. This charity aims to raise the welfare of farm and laboratory animals through the world by campaigning against cruel and unnecessary practices.

    $_____

4. This is a charity that campaigns against the imprisonment, torture and murder of innocent people living under oppressive political regimes throughout the world.

    $_____

5. This is a charity that works to rescue animals which have been abused, neglected, or ill-treated, and to find new, safe and secure homes for these animals.

    $_____

6. This charity works to help people who are suffering from chronic or terminal illnesses, by providing funding for hospices, in-home medical and nursing care, and specially equipped holiday centers.

    $_____

7. This charity works to conserve rain forests and other vital habitats in all parts of the world by campaigning against environmental destruction and pollution.

    $_____

8. This charity sends food, clothing, medicines and development aid to people all over the world who are suffering the effects of famines, natural disasters or war.

    $_____

Children's Attitudes and Behaviors towards Animals, CABTA
(Guymer et al., 2001)

Developed and Reported in:

Guymer, Elise C; Mellor, David; Luk, Ernest S.L.; Pearse, Vicky. The development of a screening questionnaire for childhood cruelty to animals. *Journal of Child Psychology and Psychiatry,* 42(8) 2001:1057–63.

Part C of the CABTA is given in Table 2, page 1059, along with response range and scoring instructions.

The authors feel that table 4, "Mean Scores on Typical and Malicious Cruelty for Males and Females by Age," and table 5, "Cutoff Scores for Cruelty to Animals and Typical and Malicious Cruelty Scores," will be of interest to users of the CABTA. These two tables are not reproduced here.

Notes:

Scoring: The CABTA enables the tester to derive three scores for the child who is the subject of his/her parent's responses. Each item in Part C is scored on a scale of 0–4 (0=left anchor, 4=right anchor). Item 18 is scored 1 for each affirmative answer.

Malicious Cruelty
Add the scores for 18a, 20, 21, 23, and 24.
Scores can range from 0–17.

Typical Cruelty
Add the scores for items 15, 16, 17, 18d, 19, and 21.
Scores can range from 0–21.

A total score is derived by adding the scores for each of the subscales scores. However, as the response to item 21 will be counted twice, it needs to be subtracted once from the summation.

Copyright Notice:

Parent/s Report of Child's Attitude and Behavior Towards Animals

This questionnaire has been developed to obtain an account of children's attitudes and behaviors towards animals. After responding to the general questions in Part A, please answer the questions in parts B and C to the best of your knowledge.

PART A

1. What is the name of your child? _____

2. What is your child's date of birth? _____

3. Do you have pets at home?   yes___ no___

4. How many pets do your family currently own? _____

5. How many pets did your family own in the past? _____

PART B

7. My child enjoys spending time with animals.

Never	Rarely	Sometimes	Often	Always

8. My child has a good relationship with our pet/s.

Not applicable	Rarely	Sometimes	Often	Always

9. My child acts in a caring manner towards our pet/s.

Not applicable	Rarely	Sometimes	Often	Always

10. My child has ridden a horse.

Not applicable	Rarely	Sometimes	Often	Always

11. My child shows responsibility for our pet/s.

Not applicable	Rarely	Sometimes	Often	Always

12. My child plays nicely with our pet/s.

| | | | | |
Not applicable Rarely   Sometimes   Often   Always

13. My child is afraid of animals.

| | | | | |
Never   Rarely   Sometimes   Often   Always

14. My child likes fishing.

| | | | | |
Never   Rarely   Sometimes   Often   Always

PART C

15. My child is rough with animals.

| | | | | |
Never   Rarely   Sometimes   Often   Always

16. My child causes harm to animals.

| | | | | |
Never   Rarely   Sometimes   Often   Always

17. The last time my child harmed an animal was

| | | | | |
Never   More than   Within the   Within the   Today
              a year ago   last year   last week

18. My child has harmed:

Small insects	yes	no
Other non-domestic animals	yes	no
Other people's pets	yes	no
His or her pet(s)	yes	no

19. My child has harmed animals alone.

| | | | | |
Never   Rarely   Sometimes   Often   Always

20. My child has harmed animals when he was with another person or in a group.

| Never | Rarely | Sometimes | Often | Always |

21. My child has harmed animals

| Never | Rarely | Sometimes | Often | Always |

22. My child has shown concern over the suffering of animals

| Never | Rarely | Sometimes | Often | Always |

23. I believe that my child has secretly harmed animals:

| Never | Rarely | Sometimes | Often | Always |

24. My child has shown pleasure when harming animals:

| Never | Rarely | Sometimes | Often | Always |

Please indicate your relationship to the child

       Mother: _____   Father: _____

       Guardian: _____   Other: _____

Your name: _____

Date: _____

Children's Treatment of Animals Questionnaire, CTAQ
(Thompson, Gullone, 2003)

Reported and validated in:

Thompson, Kelly L.; Gullone, Eleonora. The Children's Treatment of Animals Questionnaire (CTAQ): A psychometric investigation. *Society & Animals,* 11(1) 2003:1–15.

> The CTAQ assesses children's humane behavior toward animals. "The study concluded that the CTAQ is a valid and reliable measure for assessing the degree to which children's behaviour toward nonhuman animals is humane. Determining the sensitivity of the measure to change (following humane education) and the predictive validity of the measure (identification of children who are cruel to animals) will require further research" (page 1).
>
> Correlated with Bryant's Index of Empathy for Children and Adolescents, BIE (Bryant, 1982), and Social Skills Rating System, SSRS (Frank M. Gresham and Stephen N. Elliott, Social skills rating system manual [Circle Pines, Minn.: American Guidance Service, 1990]).
>
> Table 1, "The Items of the Children's Treatment of Animals Questionnaire (CTAQ)" reports 19 items, six of which were deleted from the final measure. Table 1 appears on page 6.

Notes:

Item 5 is reverse scored.

Children's Treatment of Animals Questionnaire

How often do you do the following things with your companion animal(s)?

For each statement below, please indicate whether you **never, sometimes,** or **often** do it.

Remember to mark the response that is most true for you. There are no right or wrong answers. Please do not spend too much time on any one statement.

If there are no companion animals in your home, answer in relation to other people's companion animals, or *imagine* that you have a pet. Answer the questions in relation to what you think you would do.

1.	Play with	Often	Sometimes	Never
2.	Give food or water to	Often	Sometimes	Never
3.	Take for a walk	Often	Sometimes	Never
4.	Pat	Often	Sometimes	Never
5.	Yell at	Often	Sometimes	Never
6.	Cuddle	Often	Sometimes	Never
7.	Cry with when I am sad	Often	Sometimes	Never
8.	Talk to	Often	Sometimes	Never
9.	Allow to stay in my room	Often	Sometimes	Never
10.	Play dress up with	Often	Sometimes	Never
11.	Groom	Often	Sometimes	Never
12.	Tell my secrets to	Often	Sometimes	Never
13.	Spend time with	Often	Sometimes	Never

Comfort from Companion Animals Scale, CCAS
(Zasloff, 1996)

Described in:

Zasloff, R. Lee. Measuring attachment to companion animals: A dog is not a cat is not a bird. *Applied Animal Behaviour Science,* 47(1–2) 1996 Apr:43–8.

> When the two items pertaining to dogs were included, dog owners showed a significantly higher degree of attachment. When only the eleven items pertaining to the emotional nature of the relationship were included, there were no differences in the scores of the two groups.
>
> "Table 1, Items on the Comfort from Companion Animals Scale," page 45, includes items excluded on second scoring. This article provides development and validation documentation. Construct validity is tested by correlating scores with those on the Lexington Attachment to Pets Scale, LAPS.

Developed in:

Zasloff, Ruth L.; Kidd, Aline H. Attachment to feline companions. *Psychological Reports,* 74 1994:747–52.

> An earlier version is given in Table 2, "Statements Comparing Relationships of Humans and Cats and Humans and Humans," page 749.

Used in:

Castelli, Paolo; Hart, Lynette A.; Zasloff, R. Lee. Companion cats and the social support systems of men with AIDS. *Psychological Reports,* 89(1) 2001 Aug:177–87.

> Use the CCAS, the Revised UCLA Loneliness Scale, and the General Health Questionnaire (GHQ-28).

Comfort from Companion Animals Scale

1. My pet provides me with companionship.

       1=strongly disagree   2=disagree   3=agree   4=strongly agree

2. Having a pet gives me something to care for.

       1=strongly disagree   2=disagree   3=agree   4=strongly agree

3. My pet provides me with pleasurable activity.

       1=strongly disagree   2=disagree   3=agree   4=strongly agree

4. My pet is a source of constancy in my life.

       1=strongly disagree   2=disagree   3=agree   4=strongly agree

5. My pet makes me feel needed.

       1=strongly disagree   2=disagree   3=agree   4=strongly agree

6. My pet makes me laugh and play.

       1=strongly disagree   2=disagree   3=agree   4=strongly agree

7. Having a pet gives me something to love.

       1=strongly disagree   2=disagree   3=agree   4=strongly agree

8. I get comfort from touching my pet.

       1=strongly disagree   2=disagree   3=agree   4=strongly agree

9. I enjoy watching my pet.

       1=strongly disagree   2=disagree   3=agree   4=strongly agree

10. My pet makes me feel loved.

       1=strongly disagree   2=disagree   3=agree   4=strongly agree

11. My pet makes me feel trusted.

       1=strongly disagree   2=disagree   3=agree   4=strongly agree

Companion Animal Bonding Scale, CABS

(Poresky, Hendrix, Mosier, Samuelson, 1987)

An eight-item instrument used to measure the extent of child-animal activities, CABS focuses on the quality of the relationship between the human and the pet, based on evidence that shows bonding between humans and animals can have a positive effect on humans, such as reducing feelings of alienation and loneliness.

CABS exists in two forms: contemporary form and past form, in which the verbs are, respectively, in the present and past tense. Both are reproduced.

Reported in:

Poresky, Robert H.; Hendrix, Charles; Mosier, Jacob E.; Samuelson, Marvin L. The Companion Animal Bonding Scale: Internal reliability and construct validity. *Psychological Reports,* 60(3, pt.1) 1987:743–6.

CABS is given on page 744.

". . . [CABS] is an 8-item behavioral scale describing the extent of child-animal activities. . . . The Cronbach alpha estimates of internal reliability were 0.82 and 0.77, respectively. Construct validity was indicated by significant correlations between scores on the Pet Attitude Scale [Templer et al., 1981] for the childhood and contemporary bonding scale of .39 and .40, respectively" (page 743).

". . . developed to provide an accurate measure of a person's interaction with or attachment to a pet by asking behavioral questions. . . . The CABS focuses on eight actual behaviors or events (Table 1) that an observer might see. . . . It appears to have face validity because the eight behaviors all reflect an individual's interaction with a pet. The items must be understood by the anticipated respondents. The items used in the CABS were intended for older children and adults and do not contain difficult words" (Poresky, Robert H. Analyzing human-animal relationship measures. *Anthrozoös,* 2(4) 1989:236).

Developed and validated in:

Poresky, Robert H. Analyzing human-animal relationship measures. *Anthrozoös,* 2(4) 1989:236–44.

"The Companion Animal Bonding Scale and the Companion Animal Semantic Differential meet the basic requirements described herein for internal reliability, face validity, and construct validity" (page 244).

Poresky, Robert H. The Companion Animal Bonding Scale: Internal consistency and factor structure when administered by telephone. *Psychological Reports,* 80(3) 1997 Jun:937–39.

Poresky, Robert H.; Hendrix, Charles. Young Children's Companion Animal Bonding and adults' pet attitudes: A retrospective review. *Psychological Reports,* 62 1988:412–25.

Also used in:

Andrews, Sandra Lee. The Inventory of Pet Attachment: Development and validation. 1992. x, 101 leaves. Unpublished Ph.D. thesis, Texas A&M University, 1992. Not seen. Abstract in *Dissertation Abstracts International,* Section B: The Sciences & Engineering, 53(9-B) 1993 Mar:4941-B. Not seen.

Develops the Inventory of Pet Attachment to measure non-conventional attachment to pets, and correlates scores with those on the CABS and Pet Attitude Scale (Templer et al., 1981).

Angulo, Frederick James. Pet ownership among HIV-infected persons in the Multicenter AIDS Cohort Study: Health risk or psychological benefit? 1995. xi, 51 pages. Unpublished Ph.D. thesis, University of California, Los Angeles, 1995. Not seen. Abstract in *Dissertation Abstracts International,* Section B: The Sciences & Engineering, 56(10-B) 1996 Apr:5441-B.

Angulo, Frederick J.; Siegel, Judith M.; Detels, Roger. Pet ownership and the reliability of the Companion Animal Bonding Scale among participants of the Multicenter AIDS Cohort Study. *Anthrozoös,* 9(1) 1996:5–9.

Bodsworth, Wendie; Coleman G. J. Child-companion animal attachment bonds in single and two-parent families. *Anthrozoös,* 14(4) 2001:216–33.

    Use the contemporary version of CABS. Each item was assigned a score as follows: Always = 1, Often = 2, Occasionally = 3, Rarely = 4, Never = 5 (page 218).

Brown, Julye Myner. Childhood attachment to a companion animal and social development of incarcerated male juvenile delinquents. 2000. xi, 101 pages. Unpublished Ph.D. thesis, California School of Professional Psychology, Fresno, California. Not seen. Abstract in *Dissertation Abstracts International,* Section B: The Sciences & Engineering, 60(11-B) 2000 Jun:5809-B.

    Uses the CABS, the Pet Attitude Scale (Templer et al., 1981) and the Millon Adolescent Clinical Inventory.

Bussolari, Cori Jill. The relationship among interparental conflict, animal bonding, intimate relationship satisfaction and attachment dimensions in adulthood. 2001. vi, 133 leaves. Unpublished Psy.D. thesis, University of San Francisco, 2001. Not seen. Abstract in *Dissertation Abstracts International,* Section B: The Sciences & Engineering, 62(11-B) 2002 May:5427-B.

    Uses a demographic survey, CABS, the Adult Attachment Scale (Collins & Reed, 1990), the Relationship Assessment Scale, RAS (Hendrick, 1988), and the Multidimensional Assessment of Interparental Scale, MAIC (Tschann, Flores, Pasch & Mann, 1999).

Cohen, Susan Phillips. Can pets function as family members? *Western Journal of Nursing Research,* 24(6) 2002 Oct:621–38.

    Uses the entire CABS, the complete family subscale of the Revised Kinship Scale (Nava & Bailey, 1991), 16 items of the 17-item Intimacy Scale (Walker & Thompson, 1983), four items of the 20 item UCLA Loneliness Scale (Russell, Peplau & Cutrona, 1980), four items from the 36-item Social Fear Scale (SFS; Raulin & Wee, 1984), six items from the 25-item Index of Parental Attitude (IPA; Hudson, 1982), and the Social Network Map and Grid (SNMG; Tracy & Whittacker, 1990). Small modifications in language were made to make the items applicable to pets. Modifications appear in Table 1, page 627. Scores were reversed on the CABS to make it compatible with the other scales.

Daly, Beth; Morton, L. L. Children with pets do not show higher empathy: A challenge to current views. *Anthrozoös,* 16(4) 2003:298–314.

    Use the Bryant Index of Empathy, the Questionnaire Measure of Emotional Empathy QMEE, the Pet Ownership Survey and Pet Preference Inventory, both created for this study, and the present tense CABS. "The Pet Ownership Survey . . . is a demographic questionnaire in which students indicated their grade, age, and gender, as well as the type of pet, if any, they owned. If participants owned a dog, they were asked to further describe the breed. . . . The Pet Preference Inventory . . . asks participants to rate the types of pets they would like to have (cat, horse, fish, dog, bird, and reptile) (page 303)."

Geller, Krista Scott. Quantifying the power of pets: The development of an assessment device to measure attachment between humans and companion animals. 2005. Unpublished Ph.D. thesis, Human Development, Virginia Technical Institute & State University, 2005. Not seen. Abstract available at the website http://scholar.lib.vt.edu/theses/available/etd-04252005-171588/ (accessed October 10, 2005).

Compares the CABS to the Geller Pet-Attachment Scale for the latter's validity and subjects both to factor analysis.

Nebbe, Linda Jean (Lloyd). The human-animal bond's role with the abused child. 1997. 140 leaves: illus. Unpublished Ph.D. thesis, Iowa State University, 1997. Not seen. Abstract in *Dissertation Abstracts International,* Section B: The Sciences & Engineering, 58(3-B) 1997 Sep:1568-B.

Uses the Human-Animal Bond Scale, i.e., CABS, and the Family Life Space Diagram as adapted (Barker & Barker, 1990); scales rating the subject's perception of childhood levels of self-esteem, nurturant behavior, and anger; and assessment instruments for self-esteem, nurturant behavior, and anger as an adult. The CABS "did not appropriately fit" the study population, but what "was most important was the 'perceived' relationship with the animal" [personal email communication, Nebbe, July 13, 2004].

Paskowitz, Dana Simon. The effects of human-canine interactions on pre-surgical anxiety in school-age children. 2003. xii, 159 leaves. Unpublished Ph.D. thesis, Alliant International University, California School of Professional Psychology, San Francisco Bay, 2003. Adviser: Debra Gordon. Not seen. Abstract in *Dissertation Abstracts International,* Section B: The Sciences & Engineering, 64(5-B) 2003 Nov:2399-B.

Uses Hospital Fears Rating Scale, Observer Rating Scale of Anxiety, CABS, the Companion Animal Semantic Differential, and the Human-Animal Interaction Scale.

Poresky, Robert H.; Hendrix, Charles; Mosier, Jacob E.; Samuelson, Marvin L. The Companion Animal Semantic Differential: Long and short form reliability and validity. *Educational & Psychological Measurement,* 48(1) 1988 Spring:255–60.

Correlate results from the new Companion Animal Semantic Differential (CAS) with the Pet Attitude Scale (Templer et al., 1981) and the CABS.

Poresky, Robert H. Companion animals and other factors affecting young children's development. *Anthrozoös,* 9(4) 1996:159–68.

Uses the Parental Home Assessment Index, CABS, the Iowa Social Competency Scales (Preschool Form), and an adapted Denver Prescreening Developmental Questionnaire.

Poresky, Robert H. The Young Children's Empathy Measure: Reliability, validity, and effects of companion animal bonding. *Psychological Reports,* 66(3 pt.1) 1990 Jun:931–96.

Uses Young Children's Empathy Measure, YCEM; Peabody Picture Vocabulary Test Revised, PPVT-R, and CABS.

Poresky, Robert H.; Daniels, Ann Michelle. Demographics of pet presence and attachment. *Anthrozoös,* 11(4) 1998:236–41.

Poresky, Robert H.; Hendrix, Charles. Differential effects of pet presence and pet bonding on young children. *Psychological Reports,* 67(1) 1990 Aug:51–4.

>   Use CABS, the Iowa Social Competency Scales (Preschool Form), and the Young Children's Empathy Measure.

Poresky, Robert H.; Hendrix, Charles; Mosier, Jacob E.; Samuelson Marvin L. Children's pets and adults' self-concepts. *Journal of Psychology,* 122(5) 1988:463–69.

>   In studying adults' self-concepts also administer the CABS. "Whereas gender effects were also found, no significant pet ownership or other childhood Companion Animal Bonding Scale effects were found" (abstract, page 463).

Reynolds, Theresa Evans. Pet bonding and pet bereavement as a function of culture and gender differences among adolescents. 1999. xi, 125 pages. Unpublished thesis, Ed.D, University of Sarasota, 1999. Not seen. Abstract in *Dissertation Abstracts International,* Section B: Sciences & Engineering, 60(6-B) 1999 Dec:2990-B.

>   Uses the Modified Adolescent Life Change Event Scale (ALCES), a demographic questionnaire, CABS, and a modified Texas Revised Inventory of Grief (TRIG).

Shore, Elsie R.; Petersen, Connie L.; Douglas, Deanna K. Moving as a reason for pet relinquishment: A closer look. *Journal of Applied Animal Welfare Science,* 6(1) 2003:39–52.

>   Use a human-animal bonding scale based on the CABS and the Pet Relationship Impact Inventory (Eckstein, 2000).

Taylor, Heidi; Williams, Pauline; Gray, David. Homelessness and dog ownership: An investigation into animal empathy, attachment, crime, drug use, health and public opinion. *Anthrozoös,* 17(4) 2004:353–68.

>   Use eight items from the CABS and change the wording of only two items. For example, If you were to have a pet dog at your address, would you be responsible for the dog? (Possible answers: always, often, rarely, never). Also use an adapted version of the Animal Empathy Scale (Paul, 2000).

Triebenbacher, Sandra Lookabaugh. Re-evaluation of the Companion Animal Bonding Scale. *Anthrozoös,* 12(3) 1999:169–73.

Triebenbacher, Sandra Lookabaugh. The relationship between attachment to companion animals and self-concept: A developmental perspective, pages 135–48 (Chapter 8), in: Wilson, Cindy C.; Turner, Dennis C. (editors). Companion animals in human health. Thousand Oaks, Calif.: Sage Publications, 1998. An earlier abstract of this paper appears on the Delta Society website, deltasociety.org/.

>   Uses CABS and the New York Self-Esteem Scale/Rosenberg Self-Esteem Scale (Rosenberg 1979).

Wells, Marjorie Joan. The effect of pets on children's stress responses during medical procedures. 1998. viii, 230 leaves: illus. Unpublished thesis, PhD, University of Washington, 1998. Adviser: Patricia A. Betrus. Not seen. Abstract in *Dissertation Abstracts International,* Section B: Sciences & Engineering, 59(6-B) 1998 Dec:2689-B.

Uses McNeil Pain Assessment Scale (PAS), Observational Behavioral Distress Revised (OSBD), pet history, physiological variables, CABS, and the Child Medical Fear Scale, completed by child, parent, and the health care provider.

Notes:

Also available in: Fischer, Joel; Corcoran, Kevin. *Measures for clinical practice: A sourcebook.* Vol. 1: *Couples, families, and children.* 2nd ed. New York: The Free Press, 1994, pages 457–458.

Also available in: Corcoran, Kevin; Fischer, Joel. *Measures for clinical practice: A sourcebook.* Vol. 1: *Couples, families, and children.* 3rd ed. New York: The Free Press, 2000, pages 528–529.

Also available on the Educational Testing Service website, http://sydneyplus.org/ (accessed October 22, 2004).

The total score is the sum of the answers.

The contemporary version can be obtained by changing the verb tense in each statement from past to present. Both the retrospective and contemporary versions are included here.

Copyright Notice:

Companion Animal Bonding Scale

1. How often were you responsible for your companion animal's care?

    5_____Always   4_____Generally 3_____Often   2_____Rarely   1_____Never

2. How often did you clean up after your companion animal?

    5_____Always   4_____Generally 3_____Often   2_____Rarely   1_____Never

3. How often did you hold, stroke, or pet your companion animal?

    5_____Always   4_____Generally 3_____Often   2_____Rarely   1_____Never

4. How often did your companion animal sleep in your room?

    5_____Always   4_____Generally 3_____Often   2_____Rarely   1_____Never

5. How often did you feel that your companion animal was responsive to you?

    5_____Always   4_____Generally 3_____Often   2_____Rarely   1_____Never

6. How often did you feel that you had a close relationship with your companion animal?

    5_____Always   4_____Generally 3_____Often   2_____Rarely   1_____Never

7. How often did you travel with your companion animal?

    5_____Always   4_____Generally 3_____Often   2_____Rarely   1_____Never

8. How often did you sleep near your companion animal?

    5_____Always   4_____Generally 3_____Often   2_____Rarely   1_____Never

Companion Animal Bonding Scale

1. How often are you responsible for your companion animal's care?

    5_____Always   4_____Generally 3_____Often   2_____Rarely   1_____Never

2. How often do you clean up after your companion animal?

    5_____Always   4_____Generally 3_____Often   2_____Rarely   1_____Never

3. How often do you hold, stroke, or pet your companion animal?

    5_____Always   4_____Generally 3_____Often   2_____Rarely   1_____Never

4. How often does your companion animal sleep in your room?

    5_____Always   4_____Generally 3_____Often   2_____Rarely   1_____Never

5. How often do you feel that your companion animal is responsive to you?

    5_____Always   4_____Generally 3_____Often   2_____Rarely   1_____Never

6. How often do you feel that you have a close relationship with your companion animal?

    5_____Always   4_____Generally 3_____Often   2_____Rarely   1_____Never

7. How often do you travel with your companion animal?

    5_____Always   4_____Generally 3_____Often   2_____Rarely   1_____Never

8. How often do you sleep near your companion animal?

    5_____Always   4_____Generally 3_____Often   2_____Rarely   1_____Never

Companion Animal Semantic Differential, CAS

(Poresky et al., 1988)

Reported in:

Poresky, Robert H.; Hendrix, Charles; Mosier, Jacob E.; Samuelson, Marvin L. The Companion Animal Semantic Differential: Long and short form reliability and validity. *Educational & Psychological Measurement,* 48(1) 1988 Spring:255–60.

Developed and validated in:

Poresky, Robert H. Analyzing human-animal relationship measures. *Anthrozoös,* 2(4) 1989:236–44.

"The Companion Animal Bonding Scale and the Companion Animal Semantic Differential meet the basic requirements described herein for internal reliability, face validity, and construct validity" (page 244).

Used by:

Paskowitz, Dana Simon. The effects of human-canine interactions on pre-surgical anxiety in school-age children. 2003. xii, 159 leaves. Unpublished Ph.D. thesis, California School of Professional Psychology, Alliant International University, San Francisco Bay, 2003. Adviser: Debra Gordon. Not seen. Abstract in *Dissertation Abstracts International,* Section B: The Sciences & Engineering, 64(5-B) 2003 Nov:2399-B.

Uses the Hospital Fears Rating Scale, Observer Rating Scale of Anxiety, the Companion Animal Bonding Scale, CAS, and the Human-Animal Interaction Scale.

Shiloh, Shoshana; Sorek, Gal; Terkel, Joseph. Reduction of state-anxiety by petting animals in a controlled laboratory experiment. *Anxiety, Stress, and Coping,* 16(4) 2003 Dec:387–95.

Use the State-Trait Anxiety Inventory (STAI; Spielberger, Gorsuch and Lushene, 1970) and the CAS.

Notes:

The Companion Animal Semantic Differential (CAS), a semantic differential type scale adapted from Charles E. Osgood, George J. Suci and Percy H. Tannenbaum's *The measurement of meaning* (Urbana: University of Illinois Press, 1957), attempts to accurately measure the respondent's affective perceptions of a significant childhood pet. It contains 18 bipolar word pairs describing attributes of a pet, including 11 original item pairs and seven new word pairs.

The CAS yields an internal reliability coefficient of 0.90. It also shows construct validity through its significant correlations with the Pet Attitude Scale and the Companion Animal Bonding Scale. It provides a sensitive assessment of the subject's evaluative perception of a pet. Future studies can use it to more precisely define people's attitudes toward companion animals with either the 18-item (four factor) or the more concise 9-item (single evaluative/affective factor) form.

Respondents are asked to "check the mark along the scale that describes how you felt about the pet" they had as a child. The scale has six divisions coded from 6 to 1, with eight items reversed (items 1, 3, 5, 8, 10, 13, and 17). The nine items retained in the short form (single evaluative/affective factor) are items 1, 3, 6, 7, 8, 9, 12, 13, and 17. The total score is the sum of the item responses.

Copyright Notice:

Companion Animal Semantic Differential

Check the mark along the scale that describes how you felt about the pet (companion animal) you had as a child.

1. Bad   Good

   6   5   4   3   2   1

2. Important   Unimportant

   6   5   4   3   2   1

3. Not Loving   Loving

   6   5   4   3   2   1

4. Beautiful   Ugly

   6   5   4   3   2   1

5. Hard   Soft

   6   5   4   3   2   1

6. Friendly   Not Friendly

   6   5   4   3   2   1

7. Cuddly   Not Cuddly

   6   5   4   3   2   1

8. Cold   Warm

   6   5   4   3   2   1

9. Pleasant   Unpleasant

   6   5   4   3   2   1

10.   Tense   Relaxed

     6   5   4   3   2   1

11.   Valuable   Worthless

     6   5   4   3   2   1

12.   Kind   Cruel

     6   5   4   3   2   1

13.   Bitter   Sweet

     6   5   4   3   2   1

14.   Happy   Sad

     6   5   4   3   2   1

15.   Sharp   Dull

     6   5   4   3   2   1

16.   Clean   Dirty

     6   5   4   3   2   1

17.   Distant   Close

     6   5   4   3   2   1

18.   Trusting   Fearful

     6   5   4   3   2   1

Dog Care Responsibility Inventory
(Davis, 1987)

The 18 questionnaire items pertain to the usual care and nurturing duties of family pet ownership such as feeding, grooming and physical care. Behaviors included in it are designed to be age-appropriate and are listed in alphabetical order.

Developed in:

Davis, Janet Haggerty. The role of the family dog in the preadolescent's psychosocial development relative to selected dimensions of the self-concept, sex and age. 1986. ix, 146 leaves. Unpublished Ph.D. thesis, Loyola University, Chicago, 1986. Not seen. Abstract in *Dissertation Abstracts International,* Section A: Humanities & Social Sciences, 47(11-A) 1987 May:4019-A.

> Uses the Dog Ownership History Questionnaire, the Pet/Friend Q-Sort, the Dog Care Responsibility Inventory, the Piers-Harris Children's Self-Concept Scale and Rosenberg's Perceived Self-Concept Indicators.

Used by:

Davis, Janet Haggerty. Pet care during preadolescence: Developmental considerations. *Child: Care, Health and Development,* 139(4) 1987 Jul-Aug:269–76.

> Also uses the Dog Ownership History Questionnaire (Davis, 1987).

Dog Care Responsibility Inventory

Who do you think each of these statements is most true of?

For each of these, circle one of the answers—Me, Mom, Dad, Brother or Sister.

WHO DOES THESE THINGS?

1.	First notices when dog is hungry or thirsty	Me	Mom	Dad	Bro/Sis
2.	First notices when dog is sick	Me	Mom	Dad	Bro/Sis
3.	First notices when dog wants to go out	Me	Mom	Dad	Bro/Sis
4.	Usually brushes dog	Me	Mom	Dad	Bro/Sis
5.	Usually cleans up after dog	Me	Mom	Dad	Bro/Sis
6.	Usually fixes dog's meals	Me	Mom	Dad	Bro/Sis
7.	Usually gives dog medicine or vitamins	Me	Mom	Dad	Bro/Sis
8.	Usually gives dog "treats"	Me	Mom	Dad	Bro/Sis
9.	Usually goes to the vet with dog	Me	Mom	Dad	Bro/Sis
10.	Usually looks for dog when it's lost	Me	Mom	Dad	Bro/Sis
11.	Usually makes dog behave	Me	Mom	Dad	Bro/Sis
12.	Usually plays with dog	Me	Mom	Dad	Bro/Sis
13.	Usually takes care of dog	Me	Mom	Dad	Bro/Sis
14.	Usually takes dog along when going outside	Me	Mom	Dad	Bro/Sis
15.	Usually teaches dog new things	Me	Mom	Dad	Bro/Sis
16.	Usually walks dog	Me	Mom	Dad	Bro/Sis
17.	Usually washes dog	Me	Mom	Dad	Bro/Sis
18.	Usually watches out for dog	Me	Mom	Dad	Bro/Sis

Human/Pet Relationships Measure

(Siegel, 1990)

Used in:

Siegel, Judith M. Stressful life events and use of physician services among the elderly: The moderating role of pet ownership. *Journal of Personality and Social Psychology,* 58(6) 1990:1081–6.

The Human/Pet Relationships Measure is designed to assess "four aspects of the human/pet relationship . . . responsibility, time with pet, affective attachment to pet, and benefit minus cost difference."

Reported in:

Siegel, Judith M. Companion animals: In sickness and in health. *Journal of Social Issues,* 1993:157–67, on pages 163–6.

Notes:

In the original interview version of the Human/Pet Relationships Measure, cards were prepared duplicating the possible responses to questions 4–6 and 10–12. Each card listed the possible responses. The cards, printed in large type, were handed to the subjects, all of whom were elderly, to read while the interviewer questioned them.

In asking questions 4–12, wherever "pet" is written, the interviewer mentioned instead the type of pet (cat, dog, etc.) that the subject owned.

The benefit minus cost difference is determined by subtracting the number of negative categories mentioned from the number of positive categories (for which, see pages 1082–83 in the first article listed above).

Scoring calls for two types of scores: frequencies and percentages for open-ended items (What do you like about having a pet? What do you dislike about having a pet?) and summing responses for the Likert-type items.

This measure and Siegel's research are discussed in William Langston, *Research Methods Laboratory Manual for Psychology,* 1st ed. (Pacific Grove, Calif.: Wadsworth Group, 2002), chapter 3, "Correlation Research. Stressed? Take Two Dogs and Call Me in the Morning," pages 23–32. In addition, chapter 3, supplement 2, "Additional Scales," pages 35–36, provides an adapted life events scale, pet responsibility, time spent with pet, affective attachment, and benefits and costs, from Siegel's questionnaire.

This measure is also available from the Behavioral Measurement Database Services, producer of Health and Psychosocial Instruments (HaPI) database, phone 412/687-6850; fax 412/687-5213; email: bmdshapi@aol.com for ordering information. The accession number is 18392, the title is Human/Pet Relationships Measure.

Copyright Notice:

Human/Pet Relationships Measure

1. Do you currently have any pets in your household?

> Yes ___ No ___; if **no,** skip to the concluding comment.

2. What kinds of pets do you have?

> Cat   ____
>
> Dog   ____
>
> Bird   ____
>
> Fish   ____
>
> Other (specify): _____;
>
> If respondent has more than one type of pet, ask Q.3; others skip to Q.4.

3. Which one of your pets is your favorite one? That is, the one to whom you are closest or give the most attention?

> Cat   ____
>
> Dog   ____
>
> Bird   ____
>
> Fish   ____
>
> Other (specify): _____

4. These next few questions are about your "favorite" pet. If you have a single pet, please refer to it. Thinking back to when you first got your pet, whose decision was it to get the pet? Would you say the decision was made by:

> You alone ___
>
> You and another household member ___
>
> You and someone else, or ___
>
> Someone else alone? ___

5. Who is most responsible for the care and feeding of your pet, including any trips to the veterinarian? Would you say it is:

> You alone ___
>
> You and another household member ___
>
> You and someone else, or ___
>
> Someone else alone? ___

6. When you are at home, how much of the time is your pet in the same room with you? Would you say:

    All of the time ___

    Most of the time ___

    Some of the time ___

    A little of the time, or ___

    Almost never? ___

7. About how many hours per day would you say you spend outdoors with your pet such as going for walks or just sitting in the sun?

    Number of hours/day _____

8. About how many hours a day would you say you spend petting your pet?

    Number of hours/day _____

9. About how many hours a day would you say you spend talking to your pet?

    Number of hours/day _____

10. Overall, compared to other people you know with pets, how much time would you say you spend with your pet? Would you say you spend:

    Much more time ___

    A little more time ___

    About the same amount of time ___

    A little less time or ___

    Much less time than others spend with their pets? ___

11. Would you say your pet is:

    Extremely important to you ___

    Very important to you ___

    Fairly important to you ___

    Not too important to you, or ___

    Not at all important to you? ___

12. How would you rate your pet's health overall? Would you say it is:

    Excellent ___

    Good ___

    Fair, or ___

    Poor? ___

13. What are the positive benefits of owning a pet? That is, what do you like about having a pet?

_____

_____

_____

14. What are the negative aspects of owning a pet? What do you dislike about having a pet?

_____

_____

_____

Lexington Attachment to Pets Scale, LAPS
(Johnson, Garrity, & Stallones, 1992)

Described in:

Johnson, Timothy P.; Garrity, Thomas F.; Stallones, Lorann. Psychometric evaluation of the Lexington Attachment to Pets Scale (LAPS). *Anthrozoös,* 5(3) 1992:160–75.

> The LAPS was created by using the scales from earlier work as well as items from the Companion Animal Bonding Scale (CABS; Poresky et al., 1987), the Pet Attitude Scale (PAS; Templer et al., 1981), and the Pet Attitude Inventory (Wilson, Netting & New, 1987).
>
> Table 1, Wording of LAPS Items, is on page 163.
>
> ". . . [A] final 23-question instrument . . . was developed, having excellent psychometric properties. The scale is suitable for use with dog and cat owners. Data on internal consistency, factor structure, and item response theory (IRT) modeling are presented, along with correlations between the LAPS and several domains of variables known to relate to pet attachment" (page 160).

Developed in:

Garrity, Thomas F.; Stallones, Lorann; Marx, Martin B.; Johnson, Timothy P. Pet ownership and attachment as supportive factors in the health of the elderly. *Anthrozoös,* 3(1) 1989 Summer:35–44.

> Use scales of recent life events (Appendix 1, page 44), of pet attachment (Appendix 2, page 44), of illness behavior, demographic characteristics, and the Center for Epidemiological Studies' Depression Scale (CES-D).

Stallones, Lorann; Johnson, Timothy P.; Garrity, Thomas F.; Marx, Martin B. Quality of attachment to companion animals among U.S. adults 21 to 64 years of age. *Anthrozoös,* 3(3) 1990 Winter:171–6.

> Eight items of the scale appear in Table 1, "Distribution of Responses to Pet Attachment Questions . . ."

Stallones, Lorann; Marx, Martin B.; Garrity, Thomas F.; Johnson Timothy P. Attachment to companion animals among older pet owners. *Anthrozoös,* 2(2) 1988 Fall:118–24.

Stallones, Lorann; Marx, Martin B.; Garrity, Thomas F.; Johnson, Timothy P. Pet ownership and attachment in relation to the health of U.S. adults, 21 to 64 years of age. *Anthrozoös,* 4(2) 1990 Fall:100–12.

> Use a telephone interview, which includes the LAPS, and the Center for Epidemiologic Studies Depression (CES-D) scale. Assesses illness behavior by number of physician visits and of prescription medicines used, reduction in physical activity as a result of ill health, and hospitalizations within the previous year.

Used in:

Adkins, Sherril L.; Rajecki, D. W. Pets' roles in parents' bereavement. *Anthrozoös,* 12(1) 1999:33–42.

> Use the Grief Experience Inventory (GEI; Sanders et al., 1979) and the Bereavement Experience Questionnaire (BEQ; Demi and Schroeder, 1985). Items chosen from the GEI and BEQ are reworded as needed to fit loss of a child in the past tense. Also use Videka-Sherman (1982) for coping strategies, and the LAPS.
>
> Appendix A, "Multiple-item and Single-item Pet Role Scales," page 42, presents items in a 3-point

Likert scale of Pet Helpfulness and 6-point Likert scale of Pet Role (Distraction, Comfort, Confidant, Burden, Scapegoat, Worry), both designed for this study. The points of the Pet Helpfulness scale are 1, more trouble than help; 2, made no difference; 3, helpful. See page 37.

Bagley, Debra K; Gonsman, Virginia L. Pet attachment and personality type. *Anthrozoös,* 18(1) 2005: 28–42.

Use the LAPS and the Keirsey Four Types Sorter (KFTS; Keirsey and Bates, 1978).

Brown, Sue-Ellen; Katcher, Aaron H. Pet attachment and dissociation. *Society & Animals,* 9(1) 2001:2541.

Use Dissociative Experiences Scale and the Pet Attachment Questionnaire, PAQ (1990) with a 5-point Likert Scale, never=0, seldom=1, occasionally=2, often=3, always=4.

McCutcheon, Kelly A.; Fleming, Stephen J. Grief resulting from euthanasia and natural death of companion animals. *Omega,* 44(2) 2001–2:169–88.

Use the scale from Garrity, Stallones, Marx, Johnson, Anthrozoös 3(1) 1989 Summer, Appendix B, page 44, called the Companion Animal Attachment Scale; in the abstract, it is called the Companion Animal Loss Scale.

Mogul, Marjorie. Understanding the attachment relationship between nursing home residents and resident companion animals. 2004. [120] p. Unpublished Ph.D. thesis, Bryn Mawr College, Graduate School of Social Work and Social Research, 2004. Adviser: James A. Martin. Abstract in *Dissertation Abstracts International,* Section A: Humanities & Social Sciences, 65(3-A) 2004 Sep:1120-A.

Uses the LAPS, a modified version of an Attachment Style scale, a 10-item version of the Center for Epidemiologic Studies Depression Scale, and the Activities of Daily Living Index.

Raina, Parminder; Waltner-Toews, David; Bonnett, Brenda; Woodward, Christel; Abernathy, Tom. Influence of companion animals on the physical and psychological health of older people: An analysis of a one-year longitudinal scale. *Journal of the American Geriatrics Society,* 47(3) Mar 1999:3223–9.

Use scales of Activities of Daily Living, physical impairment, psychological well-being, family and non-family social support, number of chronic conditions, number of contacts with health care professionals, and the LAPS.

Santarpio-Damerjian, Melody A. Identifying and describing the roles of companion animals in the lives of workaholics: An exploratory study of workaholism, animal companionship, and intimacy. 2002. ix, 153 leaves: ill. Unpublished Ed.D. thesis, University of Pennsylvania, 2002. Not seen. Abstract in *Dissertation Abstracts International,* Section A: Humanities & Social Sciences, 63(1-A) 2002 Jul:100-A.

Uses the Work Addiction Risk Test, Risk in Intimacy Inventory (Pilkington, Richardson, 1988), the LAPS, the Family Life Space Diagram (Barker & Barker, 1990), and a checklist of intimate behaviors developed for this study.

Shore, Elsie R.; Douglas, Deanna K.; Riley, Michelle L. What's in it for the companion animal? Pet attachment and the behaviors of college students toward their pets. *Journal of Applied Animal Welfare Science,* 8(1) 2005:1–11.

Use a survey including a demographics section, 85 questions on pet owners' behaviors, with separate sections for behaviors unique to dogs and to cats, the LAPS and a semantic differential scale (Chumley et al., 1993) (See Chumley et al., Companion animal attachment and military attachment, *Anthrozoös,* 6[4]

1993:258–73.) Four categories of pet care were used: Essential care, Standard care, Enriched care, and Luxury care.

Singer, Randall S.; Hart, Lynette A.; Zasloff, R. Lee. Dilemmas associated with rehousing homeless people who have companion animals. *Psychological Reports,* 77(3 pt.1) 1995 Dec:851–7.

Use the LAPS and the Beck Hopelessness Scale (Beck et al., 1974).

Stallones, Lorann. Pet loss and mental health. *Anthrozoös,* 7(1) 1994:43–54.

Uses demographic descriptors, Schedule of Recent Events (Holmes and Rahe, 1967), a modification of the social network index developed by Berkman (1977), the LAPS, and the Center for Epidemiologic Studies Depression (CESD) Scale.

Stammbach, Karin B.; Turner Dennis C. Understanding the human-cat relationship: Human social support or attachment. *Anthrozoös,* 12(3) 1999:162–168.

Use the LAPS, the Social Support Questionnaire (SSQ6), the Norbeck Social Support Questionnaire (NSSQ), and questionnaires assessing attachment to the cat (BrAtt) and emotional support from the cat (BrES).

Zasloff, R. Lee. Measuring attachment to companion animals: A dog is not a cat is not a bird. *Applied Animal Behaviour Science,* 47(1–2) 1996 Apr:43–8.

Correlates the Comfort from Companion Animals Scale with the LAPS.

Note:

The original LAPS scale was a telephone interview, and the interviewer read the instructions to the subject. The category "Don't Know or Refused" includes "Not Asked."

Lexington Attachment to Pets Scale

Please tell us whether you agree or disagree with some very brief statements about your favorite pet. For each statement, check whether you strongly agree, somewhat agree, somewhat disagree, or strongly disagree. You may refuse to answer.

	Agree Strongly	Agree Somewhat	Disagree Somewhat	Disagree Strongly	Don't Know or Refuse
a. My pet means more to me than any of my friends.					
b. Quite often I confide in my pet.					
c. I believe that pets should have the same rights and privileges as family members.					
d. I believe my pet is my best friend.					
e. Quite often, my feelings toward people are affected by the way they react to my pet.					
f. I love my pet because he/she is more loyal to me than most of the people in my life.					
g. I enjoy showing other people pictures of my pet.					
h. I think my pet is just a pet.					
i. I love my pet because it never judges me.					
j. My pet knows when I'm feeling bad.					
k. I often talk to other people about my pet.					
l. My pet understands me.					
	Agree Strongly	Agree Somewhat	Disagree Somewhat	Disagree Strongly	Don't Know or Refuse

	Agree Strongly	Agree Somewhat	Disagree Somewhat	Disagree Strongly	Don't Know or Refuse
m. I believe that loving my pet helps me stay healthy.					
n. Pets deserve as much respect as humans do.					
o. My pet and I have a very close relationship.					
p. I would do almost anything to take care of my pet.					
q. I play with my pet quite often.					
r. I consider my pet to be a great companion.					
s. My pet makes me feel happy.					
t. I feel that my pet is a part of my family.					
u. I am not very attached to my pet.					
v. Owning a pet adds to my happiness.					
w. I consider my pet to be a friend.					
	Agree Strongly	Agree Somewhat	Disagree Somewhat	Disagree Strongly	Don't Know or Refuse

Measurement of Pet Intervention, MOPI

(Schiro-Geist, 2001)

Created by Chrisann Schiro-Geist and her graduate assistants, MOPI evaluates the effect of animal-assisted therapy on client functioning. It has four items (attention span, physical movement, communication, and compliance) evaluated on a Likert scale of one to seven. One indicates no evidence and seven indicates strong evidence of the specified behavior. The clients are assessed over time, from beginning of the trial to the end of treatment.

Used in:

Heimlich, Kathryn. Animal-assisted therapy and the severely disabled child: A quantitative study. *Journal of Rehabilitation,* 67(4) 2001 Oct–Dec: 48–54.

> Uses the Direct Observation Form (DOF) and the Teacher's Report Form of the Child Behavior Checklists (Achenbach, 1991), the Behavior Dimensions Rating Scale (Bullock, Wilson, 1989) and the MOPI.

Heimlich, Kathryn; Schiro-Geist, Chrisann; Broadbent, Emer. Animal-assisted therapy and the child with severe disabilities: A case study. *Rehabilitation Professional,* 11(2) 2003 Apr/May/Jun:41–53.

> The case study method of reporting was selected due to a lack of methodological rigor in this study. The instruments were not subjected to tests of internal validity and reliability measures. The case study presented is believed to be representative of the changes noted across multiple participants in two groups of children studied (page 45). Table 2, Program Progress Recap, shows results of this case studfy for attention span, physical movement, communication, and compliance.

Measurement of Pet Intervention, MOPI

Evaluator: _____

Title: _____

Date: _____/_____/_____

Client: _____

Please rate the client on the following behaviors based on your interactions with the client. You are being asked to rate the client's behavior on a 7-point Likert scale where:

1 = no evidence of this behavior
7 = strong evidence of this behavior

Please circle the corresponding number:

	No evidence					Strong evidence	
Attention Span	1	2	3	4	5	6	7
Physical Movement	1	2	3	4	5	6	7
Communication	1	2	3	4	5	6	7
Compliance	1	2	3	4	5	6	7

Attention Span: This involves attention and concentration, as well as "time on task" for a particular activity; the uninterrupted time the client devotes to an activity until being distracted.

Physical Movement: This involves both gross and fine motor skills, and encompasses mobility, task-oriented movement; observably intentional movement by the client.

Communication: This involves verbal expression only; observably intentional attempts to communicate verbally by the client.

Compliance: This involves the client's following directions both implicit and direct; the completion of assigned tasks.

Comments: _____

_____

_____

Miller-Rada Commitment to Pets Scale

(Staats et al., 1996)

Described in:

Staats, Sara; Miller, Deborah; Carnot, Mary Jo; Rada, Kelly; Turnes, Jennifer. The Miller-Rada Commitment to Pets Scale. *Anthrozoös,* 9(2/3) 1996:88–93.

Appendix 1: "Pet Commitment," page 93. "[This scale] measures commitment, has high internal consistency, and correlates with attachment (r = .44)" (page 88).

Also prepared a Pet Attachment Scale, using five items from the Pet Relationship Scale (Kafer et al., 1992), four items based on previous work, and three pet problem items. This scale has good reliability (Cronbach's alpha = .89 for standard variables), reliability consistent with the PRS.

Modified in:

Shore, Elsie R.; Douglas, Deanna K.; Riley, Michelle L. Assessing the concept of commitment to pets: A comparison of the Miller-Rada Commitment to Pets Scale to two measures of pet attachment, pages 53–54, in: ISAZ 14th Annual Conference, July 11–12, 2005, Niagara Falls, NY.

Available at the website www.vetmed.ucdavis.edu/CCAB/isaz2005.pdf.

Examine the relationship between attachment, as measured by the Lexington Attachment to Pets Scale (LAPS; Johnson, Garrity, Stallones, 1992) and a single-item semantic differential attachment scale (Chumley et al., 1993, and commitment as measured by the Miller-Rada Commitment to Pets Scale. Suggest rewording the Miller-Rada Scale.

Commitment to Pets Scale

For the following questions, please circle the number representing your degree of commitment.

1=Strongly Agree   2=Agree   3=Neutral   4=Disagree   5=Strongly Disagree

1   2   3   4   5   1. If a pet destroyed a $50.00 piece of furniture or personal item, I would get rid of it.

1   2   3   4   5   2. If a pet destroyed a $4000.00 piece of furniture or personal item, I would get rid of it.

1   2   3   4   5   3. If a young pet required extensive veterinary care, I would get rid of it.

1   2   3   4   5   4. If an old pet required extensive veterinary care, I would get rid of it.

1   2   3   4   5   5. If a three month old puppy or kitten was having problems with housebreaking, I would get rid of it.

1   2   3   4   5   6. If a six month old puppy or kitten was having problems with housebreaking, I would get rid of it.

1   2   3   4   5   7. If an adult dog or cat was having problems with house breaking, I would get rid of it.

1   2   3   4   5   8. If a three month old puppy or kitten was having problems with destructiveness, I would get rid of it.

1   2   3   4   5   9. If a six month old puppy or kitten was having problems with destructiveness, I would get rid of it.

1   2   3   4   5   10. If an adult dog or cat was having problems with destructiveness, I would get rid of it.

People's Experiences Following the Death of a Pet
(Adams, 1996)

Developed in:

Adams, Cindy L. Owner grieving following companion animal death. 1996. [234] pages. Unpublished Ph.D. thesis, University of Guelph, 1996. Advisers: Brenda Bonnett, Alan Meek. Not seen. Abstract in *Dissertation Abstracts International,* Section B: The Sciences & Engineering, 57(12-B), 1997 Jun:7401-B.

Used in:

Adams, Cindy L.; Bonnett, Brenda N.; Meek, Alan H. Owner response to companion animal death: Development of a theory and practical implications. *Canadian Veterinary Journal,* 40(1) 1999 Jan:33–9.

Adams, Cindy L.; Bonnett, Brenda N.; Meek, Alan H. Predictors of owner response to companion animal death in 177 clients from 14 practices in Ontario. *Journal of the American Veterinary Medical Association,* 217(9) 2000 Nov 1:1303–9.

Lavergne, Annique G. Les déterminants de l'intensité du deuil à la suite de la perte d'un animal de compagnie: Validation d'un instrument et étude de corrélates. 2003. [158] pages. Unpublished Ph.D. thesis, Université Laval, 2003. Adviser: Michel Pépin. Not seen. Abstract published in *Dissertation Abstracts International,* Section B: Sciences & Engineering, 65(1-B) 2004 Jul:479-B.

Text in French; includes abstract in French and English and an article in English. This measure is translated into and validated in French.

People's Experiences Following the Death of a Pet
A Questionnaire

1. Date _____

2. Your name _____

3. Name of the veterinary practice where your pet was looked after

   _____

4. What is your sex? (Please circle your answer)

   1. Male

   2. Female

5. What is your age?

   _____ Years

6. What is your current marital status? (Please circle your answer)

   1. Divorced

   2. Separated

   3. Currently married

   4. Single (never married)

   5. Living with a partner

   6. Widowed

7. What is the highest level of schooling you have completed? (Please circle your answer)

   1. Less than grade 12

   2. High school

   3. College or technical school

   4. University

   5. Other (please specify) _____

8. What was your gross household income last year? (Please circle your answer)

   1. Under $15,000

   2. $15,000 to $24,999

   3. $25,000 to $49,000

   4. $50,000 and over

9. Are you working (for pay) at the present time? (Please circle your answer)

    1. yes

        If you answered **yes** to the above do you work

        1. casual (occasional work)

        2. part-time (20–24 hours a week)

        3. full-time (greater than 25 hours a week)

    2. no

10. Residence (Please circle your answer)

    1. Rural farm (hobby/production)

    2. Rural nonfarm

    3. Small town (greater than or equal to 10,000 people)

    4. City/suburb

11. What is the number of people in your household, including yourself?

    _____

Questions Regarding Your Pet

12. What was responsible for the death of your pet? (Please circle your answer)

    1. Illness

    2. Injury

    3. Old age

    4. Behavior problems

    5. Combination

13. Was your pet euthanized? (Please circle your answer)

    1. Yes

    2. No

Please place a check mark or an X on the vertical line that corresponds to your feelings for each question.

1. I was very attached to my pet.

strongly agree   agree   disagree   strongly disagree

2. In my life animals assume lower status than people.

strongly agree   agree   disagree   strongly disagree

3. If I am/was upset about the death of my pet I would remind myself that s/he was just an animal.

strongly agree   agree   disagree   strongly disagree

4. The death of my pet was a serious event in my life.

strongly agree   agree   disagree   strongly disagree

5. After my pet died I felt exhausted.

strongly agree   agree   disagree   strongly disagree

6. After the death of my pet I had difficulty sleeping.

strongly agree   agree   disagree   strongly disagree

7. After the death of my pet I had no appetite.

strongly agree   agree   disagree   strongly disagree

8. The yearning for my pet was (is) so intense that I sometimes feel physical pain in my chest.

strongly agree   agree   disagree   strongly disagree

9. Since the death of my pet I have felt as if I had a lump in my throat.

strongly agree   agree   disagree   strongly disagree

10. Since the death of my pet the hardest thing was not seeing him/her in places s/he would often be.

strongly agree   agree   disagree   strongly disagree

11. I am preoccupied with thoughts of my deceased pet.

strongly agree   agree   disagree   strongly disagree

12. I yearn for my deceased pet.

strongly agree   agree   disagree   strongly disagree

13. After the death of my pet I did not want to see any reminders of him/her (e.g., food dishes, collars, pictures).

strongly agree   agree   disagree   strongly disagree

14. Things around me still remind me of my deceased pet.

strongly agree   agree   disagree   strongly disagree

15. After the death of my pet I tried to justify what had happened.

strongly agree   agree   disagree   strongly disagree

16. I felt like there was something wrong with me because of the way I felt after the death of my pet.

strongly agree   agree   disagree   strongly disagree

17. I experienced a feeling when my pet died that something died within me.

strongly agree   agree   disagree   strongly disagree

18. After the death of my pet I tried to keep busy to take my mind off what had happened.

strongly agree   agree   disagree   strongly disagree

19. I try to avoid thinking about him/her.

strongly agree   agree   disagree   strongly disagree

20. Lessons learned, while I was growing up, about how to deal with my emotions put me in a good position to deal with the death of my pet.

strongly agree   agree   disagree   strongly disagree

21. I am so busy I hardly have time to mourn.

strongly agree   agree   disagree   strongly disagree

22. After the death of my pet I felt guilty.

strongly agree   agree   disagree   strongly disagree

23. It seems to me that the veterinarian could have done more for my pet.

strongly agree   agree   disagree   strongly disagree

24. I feel that I may have contributed to the death.

strongly agree   agree   disagree   strongly disagree

25. After my pet died it was difficult to concentrate.

strongly agree   agree   disagree   strongly disagree

26. I sometimes have difficulty believing the death has actually occurred.

strongly agree   agree   disagree   strongly disagree

27. I find it difficult to cry.

strongly agree   agree   disagree   strongly disagree

28. After the death of my pet I felt the need to cry.

strongly agree   agree   disagree   strongly disagree

29. After the death of my pet there was a change in my daily routine (e.g., I missed work).

strongly agree   agree   disagree   strongly disagree

30. Life seems emptier since the death of my pet.

strongly agree   agree   disagree   strongly disagree

31. After my pet died I felt utterly sad.

strongly agree   agree   disagree   strongly disagree

32. Life has lost its meaning since the death of my pet.

strongly agree   agree   disagree   strongly disagree

33. It is painful to recall memories of my pet.

strongly agree   agree   disagree   strongly disagree

34. At times I still feel the need to cry for my pet.

strongly agree   agree   disagree   strongly disagree

35. I still get upset when I think about the death of my pet.

strongly agree   agree   disagree   strongly disagree

36. I feel I have adjusted well to the loss of my pet.

strongly agree   agree   disagree   strongly disagree

37. Since my pet died I have obtained another pet. (Please circle your answer.)

    1. yes

    2. no

If you answered **yes** *to question 37, go to question 40.*

If you answered **no,** *begin with question 38.*

38. I plan to include another pet in my life.

strongly agree   agree   disagree   strongly disagree

39. I could not include another pet in my life at this time because of how I am feeling (about the death of my pet).

strongly agree   agree   disagree   strongly disagree

40. I know that I will/I have recovered from the death of my pet.

strongly agree   agree   disagree   strongly disagree

41. My life experience contributes to my ability to deal with the death of my pet.

     strongly agree   agree   disagree   strongly disagree

42. I dread viewing the body of a deceased animal.

     strongly agree   agree   disagree   strongly disagree

43. I think about how short life is.

     strongly agree   agree   disagree   strongly disagree

44. It does not bother me when people talk about death.

     strongly agree   agree   disagree   strongly disagree

45. I think that the future holds little for me to fear.

     strongly agree   agree   disagree   strongly disagree

46. I had concerns about what happened to my pet's body after s/he had died.

     strongly agree   agree   disagree   strongly disagree

47. It was important to me for the veterinarian to discuss the options available for the aftercare of my pet (e.g., private cremation, burial).

     strongly agree   agree   disagree   strongly disagree

48. I felt that I owed it to my pet to arrange for special care of his/her body (e.g., burial, cremation).

     strongly agree   agree   disagree   strongly disagree

49. It was important to me for the veterinarian to tell me what would happen to my pet's body after s/he died.

    strongly agree   agree   disagree   strongly disagree

50. I am preoccupied with a mental picture (image) of my deceased pet.

    strongly agree   agree   disagree   strongly disagree

51. I frequently experience angry feelings.

    strongly agree   agree   disagree   strongly disagree

52. I find myself asking "why did the death have to happen this way?"

    strongly agree   agree   disagree   strongly disagree

53. I find that I am often irritated with others.

    strongly agree   agree   disagree   strongly disagree

54. I feel anger/resentment towards some people as it relates to the death of my pet.

    strongly agree   agree   disagree   strongly disagree

55. I do not think people know how to react to a person who is grieving.

    strongly agree   agree   disagree   strongly disagree

56. Society needs to be more understanding of how people feel after their pet dies.

    strongly agree   agree   disagree   strongly disagree

57. I feel cut off and isolated.

strongly agree   agree   disagree   strongly disagree

58. I feel the need to be alone.

strongly agree   agree   disagree   strongly disagree

59. It was important to have someone to talk to after the death of my pet.

strongly agree   agree   disagree   strongly disagree

60. I feel that I can talk to people (if I need to) about how I am feeling about the death of my pet.

strongly agree   agree   disagree   strongly disagree

Please answer questions 61 through 65 if you have experienced the death of a pet in the past and then continue with question 66 and so on. If this is the first time you have experienced the loss of a companion animal, please omit questions 61–65 and begin with question 66.

61. My first experience with pet death was the most difficult for me.

strongly agree   agree   disagree   strongly disagree

62. My reaction to pet death is related to how attached I was to my pet.

strongly agree   agree   disagree   strongly disagree

63. There is a difference in how I felt following the death of pets throughout my lifetime.

strongly agree   agree   disagree   strongly disagree

64. The way that my pet died affected how I felt after s/he died.

strongly agree   agree   disagree   strongly disagree

65. Having been through the death of a pet in the past made the recent experience less difficult.

   strongly agree   agree   disagree   strongly disagree

   └_____|_____|_____|_____|_____|_____┘

66. I was surprised at how badly I felt after my pet died.

   strongly agree   agree   disagree   strongly disagree

   └_____|_____|_____|_____|_____|_____┘

67. I felt embarrassed about how I reacted following the death of my pet.

   strongly agree   agree   disagree   strongly disagree

   └_____|_____|_____|_____|_____|_____┘

68. I have experienced a critical life event in the past (death of close person, miscarriage, fatal car accident, etc.) (Please circle your answer)

   1. Yes

   2. No

If you answered **yes** *to question 68, please answer questions 69 and 70 and then continue with question 71. If you answered* **no** *to question 68, go to question 71.*

69. Having been through serious life events made me better able to deal with the death of my pet.

   strongly agree   agree   disagree   strongly disagree

   └_____|_____|_____|_____|_____|_____┘

70. Having been through other critical life events made the death of my pet seem less important.

   strongly agree   agree   disagree   strongly disagree

   └_____|_____|_____|_____|_____|_____┘

71. I am currently experiencing a serious event in my life (e.g., recent death of a close person, divorce). (Please circle your answer)

   1. Yes

   2. No

If you answered **yes** *to question 71, please answer question 72.*

If you answered **no,** *please continue with question 73.*

72. The death of my pet is more difficult because of other serious events currently taking place in my life.

strongly agree   agree   disagree   strongly disagree

If your pet was euthanized, please answer questions 73 through 85, and then continue with question 86. Otherwise, skip questions 73 through 85, and begin with question 86.

73. It did not bother me to have my pet euthanized.

strongly agree   agree   disagree   strongly disagree

74. I felt like a murderer having my pet euthanized.

strongly agree   agree   disagree   strongly disagree

75. I believe euthanasia is a good option for humanely ending the life of companion animals.

strongly agree   agree   disagree   strongly disagree

76. It was important to me if the veterinarian provided me with the option to stay with my pet during euthanasia.

strongly agree   agree   disagree   strongly disagree

77. It was/would have been helpful to have paid my bill for euthanasia on a day other than the day my pet died.

strongly agree   agree   disagree   strongly disagree

78. I felt responsible for the death of my pet.

strongly agree   agree   disagree   strongly disagree

79. After the death of my pet I felt guilty because I made a decision to euthanize my pet.

strongly agree   agree   disagree   strongly disagree

80. I felt I was rushed into making a decision to euthanize.

strongly agree   agree   disagree   strongly disagree

81. It was important to me for the veterinarian to spend time discussing whether euthanasia was the best option.

strongly agree   agree   disagree   strongly disagree

82. It was important to me for the veterinarian to spend time discussing the medical procedure of euthanasia.

strongly agree   agree   disagree   strongly disagree

83. It was important for me to spend time with my pet in the examination room after s/he died.

strongly agree   agree   disagree   strongly disagree

84. My experience following the death of my pet can be characterized as questioning whether I had made the right decision.

strongly agree   agree   disagree   strongly disagree

85. One of the hardest things about the death of my pet was leaving the veterinary clinic without my pet.

strongly agree   agree   disagree   strongly disagree

86. It was important to me to talk to the veterinarian about how I was feeling after the death of my pet.

strongly agree   agree   disagree   strongly disagree

87. I believe that the veterinarian did everything s/he could to comfort me at the time of my pet's death.

strongly agree   agree   disagree   strongly disagree

88. It was/would have been better to have paid the bill in a room other than the front reception area.

strongly agree   agree   disagree   strongly disagree

89. It was obvious, during my time at the veterinary clinic, that if I wanted to express my sadness, it was all right to do so.

strongly agree   agree   disagree   strongly disagree

90. The staff at the veterinary clinic was very supportive of how I was feeling about the death of my pet.

strongly agree   agree   disagree   strongly disagree

91. I preferred to be left alone following the death of my pet.

strongly agree   agree   disagree   strongly disagree

92. I believe that it is necessary for the veterinarian to deal with the emotions that people experience around the death of their pets.

strongly agree   agree   disagree   strongly disagree

93. The veterinarian addressed my needs around the time of the death of my pet.

strongly agree   agree   disagree   strongly disagree

94. The way the veterinary clinic handled the death of my pet helped me to cope with the death of my pet.

strongly agree   agree   disagree   strongly disagree

95. I would recommend a friend to go to this veterinary clinic because of the way the veterinarian dealt with the death of my pet.

strongly agree   agree   disagree   strongly disagree

96. The actions of the veterinarian around the time of the death of my pet make me angry/resentful.

strongly agree   agree   disagree   strongly disagree

97. It was/would have been useful to me if the veterinarian had given me more information about what people go through when their pet dies.

strongly agree   agree   disagree   strongly disagree

98. It was important for me to receive a note/card from my veterinarian after my pet died.

strongly agree   agree   disagree   strongly disagree

99. It was important to me to receive a telephone call from the veterinary clinic after my pet died.

strongly agree   agree   disagree   strongly disagree

Pet Attachment Scale—Revised
(Melson, 1988)
Pet Attachment Scale—Parent Report
(Melson, 1988)

Developed in:

Melson, Gail F. Availability of involvement with pets by children: Determinants and correlates. *Anthrozoös,* 2(1) 1988:45–52.

> The four-page Parent Report was distributed directly to parents of preschoolers and to elementary school-age children to be brought home to their parents for completion and return to the school.

Melson, Gail F.; Peet, Susan; Sparks, Cheryl. Children's attachment to their pets: Links to socio-emotional development. *Children's Environments Quarterly,* 8(2) 1991:55–65.

> The Pet Attachment Scale, designed for this study, measured affective attachment while a series of seven open-ended questions measured affective attachment, behavioral attachment, and cognitive attachment. The content of the items was adapted from the Companion Animal Bonding Scale (Poresky et al., 1987) while the format was adapted from Harter's 1982 self-concept scale.
>
> Also use the Pet Attachment Scale—Parent Report, the Index of Empathy for Children and Adolescents (Bryant, 1982), the Pictorial Scale of Perceived Competence and Social Acceptance for Young Children (Harter & Pike, 1984) or, for the fifth-grade students only, the Perceived Competence Scale for Children (Harter, 1982).

Used in:

Innes, Fiona Kirsten. The influence of an animal on normally developing children's ideas about helping children with disabilities. 1999. [208] p. Unpublished Ph.D. thesis, Purdue University, 1999. Advisers: Karen E. Diamond, Alan Beck. Portions seen. Abstract published in *Dissertation Abstracts International,* Section A: The Humanities & Social Sciences, 60(11-A) 2000 May:3897-A.

> Uses a demographic questionnaire (Appendix D), an empathy measure adapted from the work of Garner, Carlson-Jones, Miner (1994) and Hoffner & Badzinski (1989) by Diamond, Bandyk, Giorgetti, Dingel, Vaystikh (1997) consisting of vignettes with line drawings; and an assessment of their level of emotional or affective role-taking (the score sheet in Appendix F), and a slightly revised Melson's Pet Attachment Scale (1988) using line drawings of two children (examples in Appendix G) with scores from one to four (score sheet in Appendix H).

Kidd, Aline H.; Kidd, Robert M. Factors in children's attitudes toward pets. *Psychological Reports,* 66(3, Pt.1), 1990 Jun:775–86.

> Use the Melson Parent Questionnaires Activities with Pets and Interest in Pets scales, and the Pet Attitude Inventory (Wilson, Netting, New, 1987).

Vidović, Vlasta Vizek; Štetić, Vesna Vlahović; Bratko, Denis. Pet ownership, type of pet and socio-emotional development of school children. *Anthrozoös,* 12(4) 1999:211–17.

> Use the Melson "Child Pet Attachment Scale" for pet owners only, Child Empathy Scale, Child Prosocial Orientation Scale, Child Loneliness Scale, Social Anxiety Scale for Children, and Perception of Family Climate Scale.

Notes:

The following items on the Parent Attachment Scale—Parent Report are reverse scored: Shows fear of pet; Ignores pet; Gets angry or annoyed at pet; Acts insensitively toward pet; Shows dislike of pet.

Copyright Notice:

Pet Attachment Scale — Revised

Interviewer Instructions:

Tell the child that you are going to show him/her some pictures and ask him/her about his/her pet. Ask the child what kind of pet he/she has. If he/she has more than one pet, get the child to choose one of them. Note down the type of pet on the score sheet. Tell the child that you want him/her to think about this pet when he/she answers each question.

Go to the appropriate set of pictures (boy or girl with dog, cat, fish, bird, or guinea pig). For each item, read the descriptions and point at each picture while reading them, and ask the child which boy/girl is *most like* him/her. Once the child has chosen, cover the side that he/she is *least* like, and then ask him/her if he/she is *a lot* like this boy/girl or *a little bit* like this boy/girl. Point to the appropriate circle as you read each description.

On the score sheet, note down the appropriate number (indicated inside the circle) based on the circle that the child points to for each item. The warm-up item *does not* need to be scored.

A complete set of the Melson Pet Attachment Scale line drawings and text takes 120 double-sided sheets or 240 pages. Each set, for a boy with a dog, cat, fish, bird or guinea pig, or for a girl with one of these pets, consists of a warm-up item and eleven numbered items. The guinea pig can also stand in for a gerbil or small rodent. The face, which you present to the child, consists of two side-by-side pictures comparing behavior of a boy or girl with the particular pet. The back, which you see, consists of the questions and numbered balloons which match the scoring the child chooses.

What are reproduced here are reduced sets of only the boy with a dog and the girl with a dog. The text that appears on the interviewer's side of the sheet is reproduced on the left-hand side of the page; the corresponding picture appears to the right.

The same text is used with each type of pet.

The scoring sheet follows these items.

WARM-UP ITEM

This boy does not like to feed the bird.   This boy does like to feed the bird.

Which boy is more like you?

This boy?   OR   This boy?

Are you

A lot like this boy OR a little bit like this boy   A little bit like this boy OR a lot like this boy

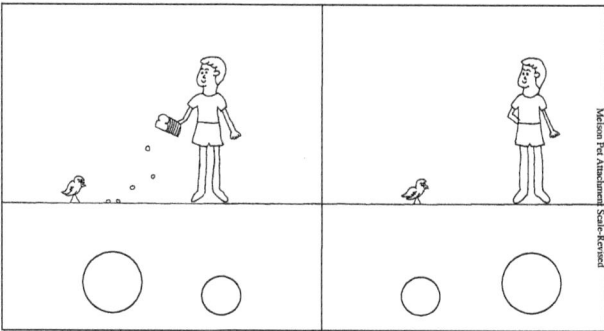

ITEM 1

This boy does take care of the pet.   This boy does not take care of the pet.

Which boy is more like you?

This boy?   OR   This boy?

Are you

A lot like this boy OR a little bit like this boy   A little bit like this boy OR a lot like this boy

4   **3**   **2**   **1**

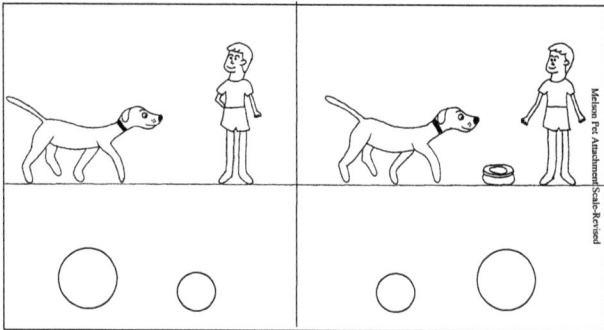

ITEM 2

This boy does clean up after the pet.   This boy does not clean up after the pet.

Which boy is more like you?

This boy?   OR   This boy?

Are you

A lot like this boy OR a little bit like this boy   A little bit like this boy OR a lot like this boy

4   **3**   **2**   **1**

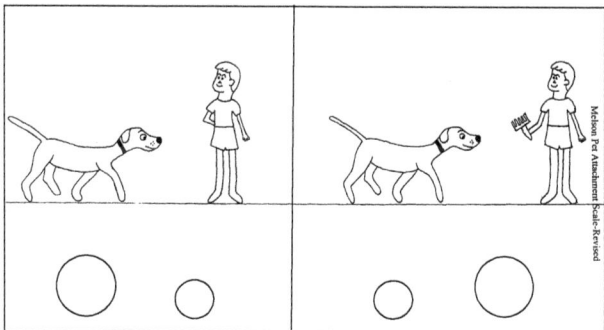

ITEM 3

This boy does not hold the pet.   This boy does hold the pet.

Which boy is more like you?

This boy?   OR   This boy?

Are you

A lot like this boy OR a little bit like this boy   A little bit like this boy OR a lot like this boy

1   **2**   **3**   **4**

ITEM 4

This boy does sleep near the pet.   This boy does not sleep near the pet.

Which boy is more like you?

This boy?   OR   This boy?

Are you

A lot like this boy OR a little bit like this boy   A little bit like this boy OR a lot like this boy

④   ③   ②   ①

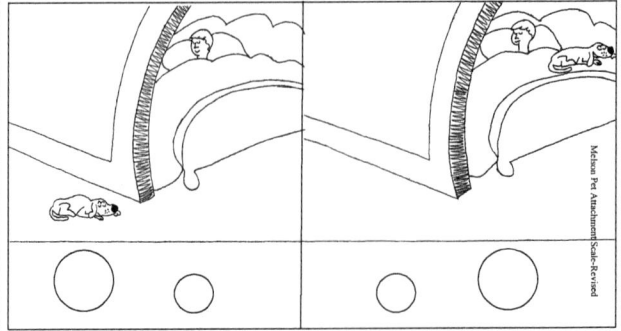

ITEM 5

This boy's pet does not know when he   This boy's pet does know he is happy.
is happy.

Which boy is more like you?

This boy?   OR   This boy?

Are you

A lot like this boy OR a little bit like this boy   A little bit like this boy OR a lot like this boy

①   ②   ③   ④

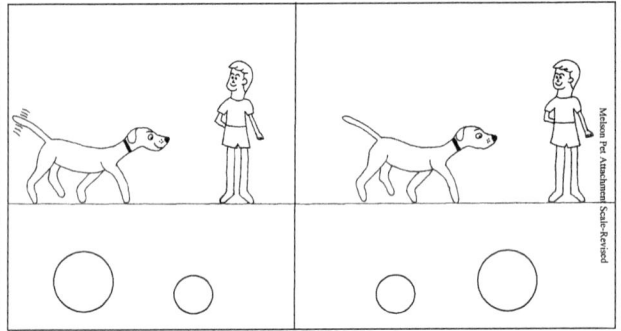

ITEM 6

This boy does not like his pet as much or   This boy does like his pet as much or
more than a good friend.   more than a good friend.

Which boy is more like you?

This boy?   OR   This boy?

Are you

A lot like this boy OR a little bit like this boy   A little bit like this boy OR a lot like this boy

①   ②   ③   ④

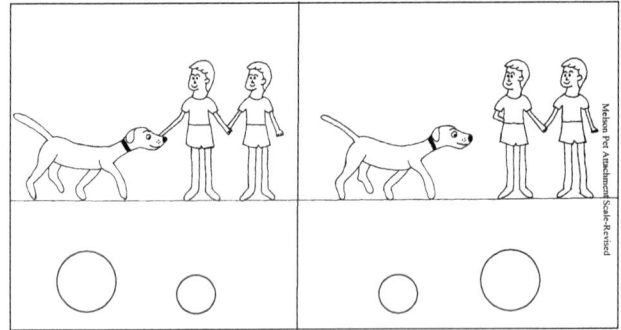

ITEM 7

This boy's pet does come on family trips.   This boy's pet does not come on family trips.

Which boy is more like you?

This boy?   OR   This boy?

Are you

A lot like this boy OR a little bit like this boy   A little bit like this boy OR a lot like this boy

④   ③   ②   ①

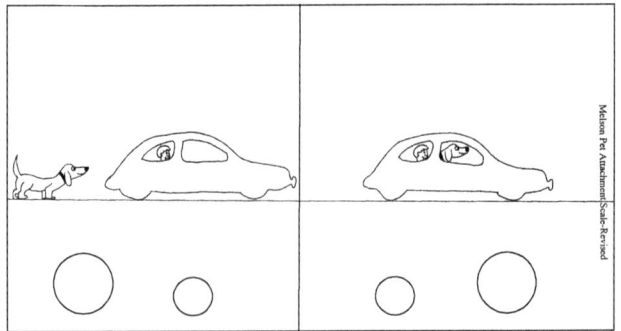

ITEM 8

This boy does not play with his pet.   This boy does play with his pet.

Which boy is more like you?

This boy?   OR   This boy?

Are you

A lot like this boy OR a little bit like this boy   A little bit like this boy OR a lot like this boy

① ② ③ ④

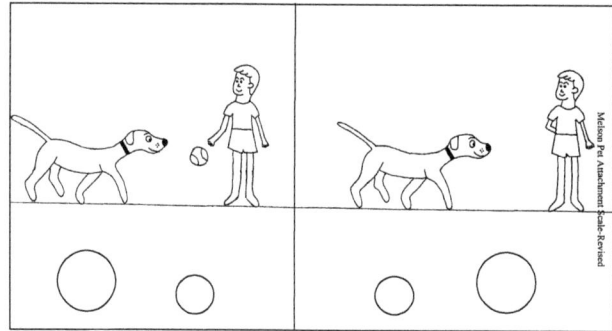

Melson Pet Attachment Scale-Revised

ITEM 9

This boy does think of his pet as a   This boy does not think of his pet as a
member of the family.   member of the family.

Which boy is more like you?

This boy?   OR   This boy?

Are you

A lot like this boy OR a little bit like this boy   A little bit like this boy OR a lot like this boy

④ ③ ② ①

Melson Pet Attachment Scale-Revised

ITEM 10

This boy did not give his pet a name.   This boy did give his pet a name.

Which boy is more like you?

This boy?   OR   This boy?

Are you

A lot like this boy OR a little bit like this boy   A little bit like this boy OR a lot like this boy

① ② ③ ④

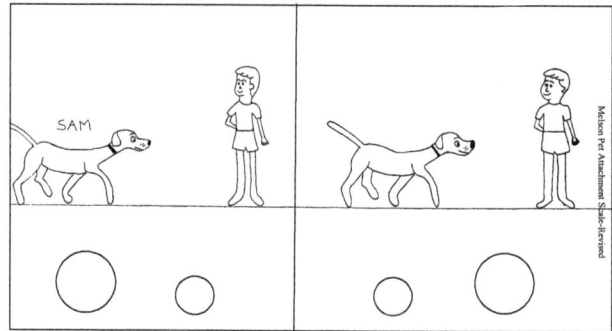

Melson Pet Attachment Scale-Revised

ITEM 11

This boy does like to give his pet gifts.   This boy does not like to give his pet gifts.

Which boy is more like you?

This boy?   OR   This boy?

Are you

A lot like this boy OR a little bit like this boy   A little bit like this boy OR a lot like this boy

④ ③ ② ①

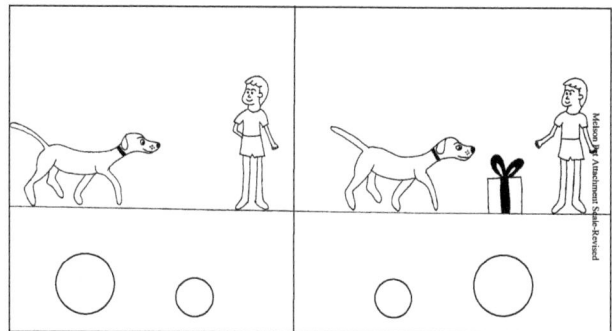

Melson Pet Attachment Scale-Revised

73

WARM-UP ITEM

This girl does not like to feed the bird.   This girl does like to feed the bird.

Which girl is more like you?

This girl?   OR   This girl?

Are you

A lot like this girl OR a little bit like this girl   A little bit like this girl OR a lot like this girl

○   ○   ○   ○

ITEM 1

This girl does take care of the pet.   This girl does not take care of the pet.

Which girl is more like you?

This girl?   OR   This girl?

Are you

A lot like this girl OR a little bit like this girl   A little bit like this girl OR a lot like this girl

(4)   (3)   (2)   (1)

○   ○   ○   ○

ITEM 2

This girl does clean up after the pet.   This girl does not clean up after the pet.

Which girl is more like you?

This girl?   OR   This girl?

Are you

A lot like this girl OR a little bit like this girl   A little bit like this girl OR a lot like this girl

(4)   (3)   (2)   (1)

○   ○   ○   ○

ITEM 3

This girl does not hold the pet.   This girl does hold the pet.

Which boy is more like you?

This boy?   OR   This boy?

Are you

A lot like this girl OR a little bit like this girl   A little bit like this girl OR a lot like this girl

(1)   (2)   (3)   (4)

○   ○   ○   ○

ITEM 4

This girl does sleep near the pet.   This girl does not sleep near the pet.

Which girl is more like you?

This girl?   OR   This girl?

Are you

A lot like this girl OR a little bit like this girl   A little bit like this girl OR a lot like this girl

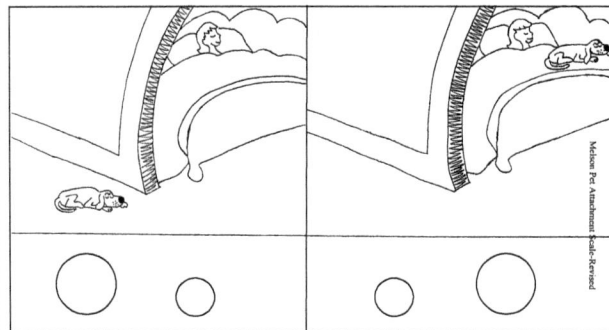

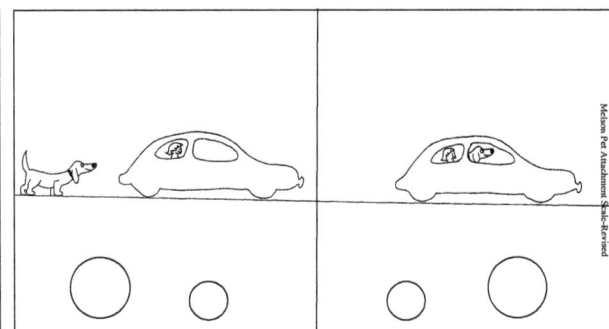

(4)   (3)   (2)   (1)

ITEM 5

This girl's pet does not know when she   This girl's pet does know she is happy.
is happy.

Which girl is more like you?

This girl?   OR   This girl?

Are you

A lot like this girl OR a little bit like this girl   A little bit like this girl OR a lot like this girl

(1)   (2)   (3)   (4)

ITEM 6

This girl does not like her pet as much or   This girl does like her pet as much or
more than a good friend.   more than a good friend.

Which girl is more like you?

This girl?   OR   This girl?

Are you

A lot like this girl OR a little bit like this girl   A little bit like this girl OR a lot like this girl

(1)   (2)   (3)   (4)

ITEM 7

This girl's pet does come on family trips.   This girl's pet does not come on family trips.

Which girl is more like you?

This girl?   OR   This girl?

Are you

A lot like this girl OR a little bit like this girl   A little bit like this girl OR a lot like this girl

(4)   (3)   (2)   (1)

ITEM 8

This girl does not play with her pet.   This girl does play with her pet.

Which girl is more like you?

This girl?   OR   This girl?

Are you

A lot like this girl OR a little bit like this girl   A little bit like this girl OR a lot like this girl

1   2   3   4

ITEM 9

This girl does think of her pet as a member of the family.   This girl does not think of her pet as a member of the family.

Which girl is more like you?

This girl?   OR   This girl?

Are you

A lot like this girl OR a little bit like this girl   A little bit like this girl OR a lot like this girl

4   3   2   1

ITEM 10

This girl did not give her pet a name.   This girl did give her pet a name.

Which girl is more like you?

This girl?   OR   This girl?

Are you

A lot like this girl OR a little bit like this girl   A little bit like this girl OR a lot like this girl

1   2   3   4

ITEM 11

This girl does like to give her pet gifts.   This girl does not like to give her pet gifts.

Which girl is more like you?

This girl?   OR   This girl?

Are you

A lot like this girl OR a little bit like this girl   A little bit like this girl OR a lot like this girl

4   3   2   1

Pet Attachment Scale

ID# _____

Interviewer: Write down the type of pet that the child has. If he/she has more than one pet, get him/her to choose one. If he/she doesn't have a pet, write "none" in the space below. For each item, write down the appropriate number.

Type of pet: _____

Item 1:	4	3	2	1
Item 2:	4	3	2	1
Item 3:	4	3	2	1
Item 4:	4	3	2	1
Item 5:	4	3	2	1
Item 6:	4	3	2	1
Item 7:	4	3	2	1
Item 8:	4	3	2	1
Item 9:	4	3	2	1
Item 10:	4	3	2	1
Item 11:	4	3	2	1

Pet Attachment Scale—Parent Report

Instructions: Please complete all of the following items as accurately as possible.
Your answers are strictly confidential. If you have more than one child, please answer the items about the child who is participating in the study.

Does your household currently own a pet? ___yes ___ no   (circle one)

If you answered **no** to this question, please return the questionnaire to the labeled folder in your child's classroom. If you answered yes to this question, please complete the rest of the questionnaire.

In our interview with your child, he/she answered questions about your _____. For consistency, please complete the following items in regard to your child and your _____.

For each of the items below, please estimate the *amount of time* your child spends on each of the following pet-related activities.

   1 = Never
   2 = Rarely (less than once a month)
   3 = Occasionally (several times a month)
   4 = Regularly (several times a week)
   5 = Often (almost every day or whenever needed)

Feeds pet	1	2	3	4	5
Cleans or grooms pet	1	2	3	4	5
Walks pet	1	2	3	4	5
Teaches pet	1	2	3	4	5
Disciplines pet	1	2	3	4	5
Observes pet	1	2	3	4	5
Talks to pet	1	2	3	4	5
Shows fear of pet	1	2	3	4	5
Shows affection to pet	1	2	3	4	5
Cares for living area (e.g., cage, litter)	1	2	3	4	5
Sleeps near pet (in same room)	1	2	3	4	5
Trains pet	1	2	3	4	5
Plays with pet	1	2	3	4	5

During the last month, please estimate the *amount of time* your child has shown each of the following expressions of interest in pets. Please use the following scale:

1 = Never

2 = Rarely (less than once a month)

3 = Occasionally (several times a month)

4 = Regularly (several times a week)

5 = Often (almost every day or whenever needed)

Please circle the number that is the best answer.

Talks about pet	1	2	3	4	5
Wants to care for pet	1	2	3	4	5
Ignores pet	1	2	3	4	5
Wants to play with pet	1	2	3	4	5
Wants another pet	1	2	3	4	5
Shows concern about pet	1	2	3	4	5
Gets angry or annoyed at pet	1	2	3	4	5
Expresses ownership of pet	1	2	3	4	5
Shows protective behavior of pet	1	2	3	4	5
Acts insensitively toward pet	1	2	3	4	5
Wants to sleep with pet	1	2	3	4	5
Shows dislike of pet	1	2	3	4	5
Talks to pet	1	2	3	4	5
Expresses love and affection to pet	1	2	3	4	5

Some children are given responsibility for some care or involvement with a pet, while other children are not. Please circle the appropriate number for each item below.

1 = Never
2 = Rarely (less than once a month)
3 = Occasionally (several times a month)
4 = Regularly (several times a week)
5 = Often (almost every day or whenever needed)

Please circle the number that is the best answer.

My child is responsible for feeding the pet.	1	2	3	4	5
My child is responsible for cleaning the pet.	1	2	3	4	5
My child is responsible for disciplining the pet.	1	2	3	4	5
My child is responsible for exercising the pet.	1	2	3	4	5

Is there anything else you would like to tell us about your child's involvement with a pet or pets?

Pet Attitude Inventory, PAI
(Wilson, Netting & New, 1987)

Wilson, Cindy C.; Netting, F. Ellen; New, John C. The Pet Attitude Inventory. *Anthrozoös,* 1(2) 1987 Fall:76–84.

"The Pet Attitude Inventory for Pet Owners," pages 79–82; "The Pet Attitude Inventory for Non-Pet Owners," pages 83–84. A two-track instrument, designed for owners and non-owners for use in community settings. The PAI is intended to measure pet ownership attitudes and attachment levels and answer questions related to the fields of medicine, psychology, social work, and aging. Its strengths include attention to the concept of life-span development, ease of administration, and attention to housing. It has content validity as determined by experts in public health, veterinary medicine, psychology, social work, and aging, but it has not been tested for reliability. It contains both open and forced-choice questions and can be interviewer- or self-administered in about five to ten minutes.

Developed in:

Netting, F. Ellen; Wilson, Cindy C.; New, John C. Developing a multidisciplinary pet placement program for community-based elderly. *Journal of Applied Gerontology,* 3(2) 1984 Dec:181–191.

Developed with a functional assessment inventory that evaluates the level of client functioning.

Wilson, Cindy C.; Netting, F. Ellen; New, John C. Developing the Pet Attitude Inventory: Measuring the human-animal bond. *California Veterinarian,* 39(3) 1985 May/Jun:26–28.

Describe development of the PAI and reports preliminary reliability data.

Also used in:

Johnson, Rebecca A.; Meadows, Richard L. Older Latinos, pets, and health. *Western Journal of Nursing Research,* 24(6) 2002 Oct:609–20.

Use the Demographic Questionnaire (DQ), the Pet Relationship Scale (PRS), 20 items of the Pet Attitude Inventory, the Iowa Self Assessment Inventory (ISAI), and the Self-Perceived Health Questionnaire.

Kidd, Aline H.; Kidd, Robert M. Factors in adults' attitudes toward pets. *Psychological Reports,* 65 1989:903–10.

Marks, Shaela G.; Koepke, Jean E.; Bradley, Cheryl L. Pet attachment and generativity among young adults. *Journal of Psychology,* 128(6) 1994 Nov:641–50.

Use the PAI, the CENSHARE Pet Attachment Survey (Holcomb et al., 1985), and the Loyola Generativity Scale (LGS; McAdams, de St. Aubin, 1992).

Netting, F. Ellen; Wilson, Cindy C.; Fruge, Charles. Pet ownership and nonownership among elderly in Arizona. *Anthrozoös,* 2(2) 1988 Fall:125–32.

Modified the PAI to elicit information on the respondent's pet history to obtain a life-span perspective.

New, John C, Jr.; Wilson, Cindy C.; Netting, F. Ellen. How community-based elderly perceive pet owner-ship. *California Veterinarian,* 40(5) 1986 Oct:22–7.

Robertson, Jessie C; Gallivan, Joanne; MacIntyre, Peter D. Sex differences in the antecedents of animal use attitudes. *Anthrozoös,* 17(4) 2004:306–19.

Use some of the statements from the PAI and develop others for the Pet Care Experience and Pet Attach-ment Scale (Table 2, page 319).

Notes:

The Pet Attitude Inventory (PAI) was abandoned shortly after it was reported in Anthrozoös and was not de-veloped further. The authors feel that other researchers have developed better instruments with published re-liability and validity data. They do not feel that the PAI is best for most research being conducted or planned today (personal communication from John C. New, Jr., October 23, 2003). However, the PAI is reproduced here to contribute to the completeness of this book, in the expectation that some might find it a good starting place.

Copyright Notice:

Pet Attitude Inventory for Pet Owners

Directions:

Circle the appropriate response. Please complete all questions.

Demographic Information

"Do you have a pet now?"

*(If **yes,** continue. If **no,** use the Pet Attitude Inventory for Non-pet Owners.)*

1. What is your sex?

    1. Female

    2. Male

2. What is your race?

    1. Black

    2. White

    3. Hispanic

    4. Native American

    5. Asian

    6. Other, specify _____

3. On your last birthday, how old were you?

    _____

4. What is your marital status?

    1. Divorced or Separated

    2. Married

    3. Never Married

    4. Widowed

5. What is the highest level (in years) that you completed in school?

    1. 0–6 years

    2. 7–9 years

    3. 10–11 years

    4. High School Graduate

    5. College, 1–3 Years

    6. College Graduate

    7. Postgraduate

6. In what kind of housing do you live?

    1. Single Family

    2. Apartment

    3. Trailer

    4. Townhouse/Condo

    5. Institutional Setting (e.g., nursing home)

    6. Other _____

7. How would you rate your health at present?

    1. Excellent

    2. Good

    3. Fair

    4. Poor

Pet Survey

1. Did you grow up with pets?

    1. Yes

    2. No

1a. If **yes,** what kinds of pets?

    1. Birds

    2. Cats

    3. Dogs

    4. Other _____

2. When did you first have responsibility for the care of the pet? If the answer is NEVER, skip to #3.

    1. Childhood (1–12 yrs)

    2. Adolescence (13–18 yrs)

    3. Young adulthood (19–30 yrs)

    4. Middle age (31–61 yrs)

    5. Old age (62 and older)

    6. Never

2a. What kind of pet was it?

    1. Bird

    2. Cat

    3. Dog

    4. Other _____

2b. How attached were you to this pet?

    1. Very attached

    2. Attached

    3. Not very attached

2c. What happened to this pet?

    1. Died

    2. Gave it away. Reason:_____

    3. Ran away (disappeared)

    4. Other _____

2d. Was this pet replaced?

    1. Yes

    2. No

3. At what stages of your life did you have pets? Circle all that apply.

    1. Childhood (1–12 yrs)

    2. Adolescence (13–18 yrs)

    3. Young adulthood (19–30 yrs)

    4. Middle age (31–61 yrs)

    5. Old age (62 yrs and older)

4. Do you have any dogs, cats or birds now?

    1. Yes

    2. No

    *If **no,** use Pet Attitude Inventory for Non-pet Owners*

5. How many do you have now? If only one pet, skip to #7.

    _____ Birds

    _____ Cats

    _____ Dogs

6. If you have more than one pet now, which one are you most attached to? If you cannot choose a favorite, choose the animal you have had the LONGEST. The rest of the questions are only about this pet.

    1. Bird

    2. Cat

    3. Dog

7. What is the name of this pet? _____

8. Why did you give it this name?

    1. Don't know why I named it that.

    2. First name that came to mind.

    3. It looked like its name (For example, Spot because it had spots).

    4. Named it after a friend or relative.

    5. To explain a characteristic (For example, he was always getting in trouble, so I named him Trouble).

    6. Was already named when I got it.

    7. Other _____

9. Have you ever had another pet with this name?

    1. Yes

    2. No

10. Is it male or female? If pet is a bird, skip to #12.

    1. Female

    2. Male

    3. Don't know

11. Is it neutered (fixed)? This question applies to both male and female pets. *If* **no,** *go to #11a.*

    1. Yes

    2. No

    3. Don't know

11a. If **no,** what was the primary reason? *If questions are about the pet you have had the LONGEST, skip to #13.*

    1. No reason

    2. Don't like the idea

    3. It makes them fat

    4. It makes them lazy

    5. Never allowed outside the house or yard

    6. Too expensive

    7. Too much trouble

    8. Other _____

This next question is only for owners with more than one pet.

12. Of the pets currently owned, is this pet the one you have had the longest?

    1. Yes

    2. No

13. How long have you had this pet?

    1. Less than one year

    2. 1–5 years

    3. 6–10 years

    4. More than 10 years

14. How old is your pet now?

    1. Less than one year old

    2. 1–5 years old

    3. 6–10 years old

    4. More than 10 years old

15. How did you get this pet? What was the source of this pet?

    1. Adopted from animal shelter or pound

    2. Born to a pet I already had

    3. Bought the pet myself (or by my spouse)

    4. Gift to me

    5. Stray (just showed up)

    6. Other _____

16. People have different attachments to their pets. How attached are you to your pet?

    1. Very attached

    2. Attached

    3. Not very attached

17. How often does your pet stay inside your residence?

    1. Always stays inside   If "1"or "2", skip to #19.

    2. Frequently inside

    3. Seldom comes inside

    4. Never comes inside

18. If the pet seldom or never comes inside, do you have a fenced-in yard?

    1. Yes

    2. No

19. Who usually takes the most care of this pet?

    1. Friend or relative not living in household

    2. Other household member

    3. Yourself

20. How much time, on an average daily basis, do you spend doing something with or for your pet, such as grooming it, petting it, walking or feeding it? This does not mean just being in the same room.

    1. One hour or less

    2. More than one hour

21. Is the time spent in these activities

    1. Enjoyable?

    2. Not enjoyable?

    3. Sometimes enjoyable, sometimes not?

22. Does touching your pet

    1. Make you feel better?

    2. Make no difference in how you feel?

    3. Make you feel worse?

23. When you physically feel bad, does your pet

    1. Make you feel better?

    2. Make no difference in how you feel?

    3. Make you feel worse?

24. When you are feeling sad, does your pet

    1. Make you feel better?

    2. Make no difference in how you feel?

    3. Make you feel worse?

25. If you were to take a trip, would you most likely

    1. Board the pet?

    2. Find someone who would care for the pet in their home?

    3. Have someone come in to care for the pet?

    4. Take the pet with you?

    5. Other _____

26. Do you worry about your pet's future if something happened to you?

    1. Yes

    2. No

27. If you were hospitalized, who would take care of your pet?

    1. Family

    2. Friend (includes neighbors)

    3. No one

    4. Other _____

28. If you could find someone who would care for your pet in a loving manner, would you give it up?

    1. Yes

    2. No

    3. Don't know

29. Do you talk to your pet?

    1. Yes   *If* **yes,** *go to #29a.*

    2. No

29a. If **yes,** WHEN do you talk to your pet? Circle all that apply.

    1. When I am upset.

    2. When I am happy

    3. When there is no one else to talk to.

    4. Other _____

29b. How often do you talk to your pet?

    1. A lot

    2. A little

29c. Does your pet respond when you talk to it?

    1. Yes

    2. No

30. Do you confide in your pet?

    1. Yes   *If* **yes,** *go to #30a.*

    2. No

30a. If **yes,** do you confide in your pet more easily than in a person?

    1. Yes   *If* **yes,** *go to #30b.*

    2. No

30b. If **yes,** why?

    1. Does not judge me.

    2. Does not talk back to me.

    3. Loves me regardless of what I say.

    4. No one else to talk to.

    5. Other _____

31. Have you met new people because of your pet? (For example, do you talk to your neighbors when you are out walking your dog?)

    1. Yes   *If* **yes,** *go to #31a.*

    2. No

31a. If **yes,** how many different people within a month's time?

    _____ (Number of people)

32. Do you talk with other people about your pet? (For example, if someone is visiting your house, is your pet a topic of the conversation?)

    1. Yes

    2. No

33. How much companionship does your pet give you?

    1. A lot

    2. A little

    3. None

34. If your pet died, would you get another pet?

    1. Yes

    2. No

    3. Maybe

35. Is owning your pet a burden?

    1. Always

    2. Sometimes

    3. Never   *If* **never,** *skip to #36.*

35a. If **always** or **sometimes,** why?

    1. Costs too much

    2. Is a nuisance

    3. Hard to get to veterinarian for medical care

    4. Tears things up

    5. Other _____

36. What is your reason(s) for having a pet? Circle all that apply.

    1. I enjoy (love) animals

    2. I wanted a pet for protection.

    3. I wanted some companionship.

    4. I wanted something I could take care of.

    5. I wanted something to keep me busy (occupy the time).

    6. I was given this pet.

    7. Other _____

36a. Which reason is **most** important?

    _____

    (Enter number from above)

Closing Remarks

Thank you for taking part in this project. Your cooperation has helped to make it a success and will help us add to the knowledge about people and their pets. Do you have any questions that you would like to ask?

Pet Attitude Inventory for Non-pet Owners

Directions:

Circle the appropriate response. Please complete all questions. Do not leave questions unanswered.

Demographic Information

1. What is your sex?

    1. Female

    2. Male

2. What is your race?

    1. Black

    2. White

    3. Hispanic

    4. Native American

    5. Asian

    6. Other, specify _____

3. On your last birthday, how old were you?

    _____

4. What is your marital status?

    1. Divorced or Separated

    2. Married

    3. Never Married

    4. Widowed

5. What is the highest level (in years) that you completed in school?

    1. 0–6 years

    2. 7–9 years

    3. 10–11 years

    4. High School Graduate

    5. College, 1–3 Years

    6. College Graduate

    7. Postgraduate

6. In what kind of housing do you live?

    1. Single Family

    2. Apartment

    3. Trailer

    4. Townhouse/Condo

    5. Institutional Setting (e.g., nursing home)

    6. Other _____

        (Handle by hand)

7. How would you rate your health at present?

    1. Excellent

    2. Good

    3. Fair

    4. Poor

Pet Survey

1. Have you ever had a dog, cat or bird? If **no**, skip to question #5.

    1. Yes

    2. No

2. What was the last time you had a pet?

    1. Less than one year

    2. 1–5 years ago

    3. 6–10 years ago

    4. Greater than 10 years ago

3. What kind of pet was it?

    1. Bird

    2. Cat

    3. Dog

    4. Other, specify_____

4. What happened to your pet?

    1. Died

    2. Gave it away. Reason:_____

    3. Ran away (disappeared)

    4. Other _____

5. How much does it bother you that you do not have a pet?

    1. A lot

    2. A little

    3. Not at all

6. What are your reasons for not having pets now? Circle all that apply.

    1. I am allergic to animals.

    2. I can't keep a pet at my present residence.

    3. I couldn't afford the cost of a pet.

    4. I couldn't physically handle the demands of taking care of a pet.

    5. I don't enjoy animals.

    6. I don't want to be bothered having to care for a pet.

    7. Other household members are allergic to animals.

    8. Other household members do not like animals.

    9. Other _____

6a. Which of those reasons circled above is your MOST important reason for not having a pet?

    _____   If "**2**," go to #6b. If "**3**," skip to #6c.

    (Enter number from above)   If any other response given, skip to #7.

6b. If the situation were changed and you could have pets in your residence, would you want a pet?

    1. Yes   If **yes,** skip to #7.

    2. No   If **no,** skip to closing remarks.

6c. If you could afford the cost of a pet, would you want one?

    1. Yes   If **yes,** go to #7.

    2. No   If **no,** skip to closing remarks.

7. Do you have any reason(s) for getting a pet in the near future? Circle all that apply.

    1. A family member or friend wants to give me a pet.

    2. I enjoy (love) animals.

    3. I have always had a pet.

    4. I have more time now to care for a pet.

    5. I need something to care for.

    6. I want a pet for protection.

    7. I would like a pet to keep me busy.

    8. I would like some more companionship.

    9. Other _____

7a. Which of those circled would be your MOST important reason?

_____ If no reasons stated, skip to closing remarks.

   (Enter number from above)

8. What kind of pet would you consider?

   1. Bird

   2. Cat

   3. Dog

   4. Other, specify_____

9. How much could you afford to spend on a pet per month?

   1. Less than $10.00

   2. $10.00–$20.00

   3. Over $20.00

10. Do you have any worries or concerns about caring for a new pet?

   1. Yes

   2. No   If **no,** skip to #11.

10a. If **yes,** what are your major concerns? Circle all that apply.

   1. Housebreaking it.

   2. I would get too attached to it.

   3. It would cause me to fall or trip.

   4. It would get sick and I would not be able to get it medical care.

   5. It would make too much noise.

   6. It would tear things up.

   7. Something might happen to me and no one would care for it.

   8. Other _____

11. If it is possible, would you consider letting us place a pet with you on a trial basis?

   1. Yes

   2. No

Closing Remarks

Thank you for taking part in this project. Your cooperation has helped to make it a success and will help us add to the knowledge about people and their pets. Do you have any questions that you would like to ask?

Pet Attitude Scale—Modified, PAS-M
(Templer et al., 1981; Munsell et al., 2004)

Reported in:

Templer, Donald I.; Salter, Charles A.; Dickey, Sarah; Baldwin, Roy; Veleber, David M. The construction of a Pet Attitude Scale. *Psychological Record,* 31(3) 1981 Summer:343–48.

Also use the Marlowe-Crowne Social Desirability Scale and an acquiescent response measure of Couch and Keniston (1960).

Table 1, page 344, reproduces the 18-item Pet Attitude Scale items and key.

Modified in:

Munsell, Kathleen L.; Canfield, Merle; Templer, Donald I.; Tangan, Kimberly; Arikawa, Hiroko. Modification of the Pet Attitude Scale. *Society & Animals,* 12(2) 2004:137–42.

Use both the 1981 PAS and the modified, 2004 PAS. The recommended modifications are presented here.

This study is available on the Society and Animals Forum website www.societyandanimalsforum.org.

Comments:

The PAS "is one of the few published scales with reliability information (Cronbach alpha of .93, and two-week test-retest stability of .92) in the undergraduate sample (N=92) used to develop the scale. The PAS contains 18 items that represent three factorially derived subscales: 'love and interaction,' 'pets in the home,' and 'joy of pet ownership.'" Lago et al. (1988). Assessment of favorable attitudes toward pets: Development and preliminary validation of self-report pet relationship scales. *Anthrozoös,* 1(4) 1988 Summer:41–42.

Also used by:

Al-Fayez, Ghenaim; Awadalla, Abdelwahid; Templer, Donald I.; Arikawa, Hiroko. Companion animal attitude and its family pattern in Kuwait. *Society & Animals,* 11(1) 2003:17–28.

Allen, Karen M.; Blascovich, Jim; Tomaka, Joe; Kelsey, Robert M. Presence of human friends and pet dogs as moderators of autonomic responses to stress in women. *Journal of Personality and Social Psychology,* 61(4) 1991 Oct:582–89.

Use the 1981 PAS and a questionnaire assessing data about pet ownership.

Andrews, Sandra Lee. The Inventory of Pet Attachment: Development and validation. 1992. x, 101 leaves. Unpublished Ph.D. thesis, Texas A&M University, 1992. Not seen. Abstract in *Dissertation Abstracts International,* Section B: The Sciences & Engineering, 53(9-B) 1993 Mar:4941-B.

Develops and validates the IPA for nonconventional attachment to pets and correlates scores with the 1981 PAS and the Companion Animal Bonding Scale (Poresky et al., 1987).

Brown, Julye Myner. Childhood attachment to a companion animal and social development of incarcerated male juvenile delinquents. 1999. x, 101 pages: illus. Unpublished Ph.D. thesis, California School of

Professional Psychology-Fresno, 1999. Not seen. Abstract in *Dissertation Abstracts International,* Section B: The Sciences & Engineering, 60(11-B) 2000 May:5809-B.

Uses the Companion Animal Bonding Scale, the 1981 PAS, and the Millon Adolescent Clinical Inventory.

Charnetski, Carl J.; Brennan, Francis X. In praise of pets: Your immune system's best friend, pages 121–39, in Charnetski, Carl J.; Brennan, Francis X. *Feeling good is good for you.* [Emmaus, PA]: Rodale Press, 2001. xiii, 209 p.

The 1981 PAS is reproduced in full with a 7-point Likert scale as "Your animal instincts," pages 130–33. The authors tell the reader how to take the test and interpret the results.

Charnetski, Carl J.; Riggers, Sandra; Brennan, Francis X. Effect of petting a dog on immune system function. *Psychological Reports,* 95 2004:1087–91.

Use the 1981 PAS.

Chumley, Perry R.; Gorski, June D.; Saxton, Arnold M.; Granger, Ben P.; New, John C., Jr. Companion animal attachment and military transfer. *Anthrozoös,* 6(4) 1993:258–73.

The authors combine Pet Relationship Scales 1 and 2 (less item 10) and seven items from the PAS to form a 21-item Pet Attachment Survey with a 6-point Likert scale. This "Survey for Military Companion Animal Owners" (i.e., the Pet Attachment Scale) is published on pages 272–73.

Cox, Ruth P. The human/animal bond as a correlate of family functioning. *Clinical Nursing Research,* 2(2) 1993 May:224–31.

Uses the Family Adaptability and Cohesion Evaluation Scale, FACES III (Olson, Portner and Lavee, 1985), and the 1981 PAS.

Crowley-Robinson, Patricia; Blackshaw, Judith K. Nursing home staffs' empathy for a missing therapy dog, their attitudes to animal-assisted therapy programs and suitable dog breeds. *Anthrozoös,* 11(2) 1998:101–4.

Use a questionnaire on staff attitudes to animal-assisted therapy programs and the 1981 PAS.

Esparza, Jana Scoville. Personality characteristics associated with pet ownership: Validating the theoretical propositions of Boris Levinson. 1990. iv, 94 leaves. Unpublished Ph.D. thesis, University of North Texas, 1990. Not seen. Abstract in *Dissertation Abstracts International,* Section B: The Sciences & Engineering, 51(10-B) 1991 Apr:5026-B.

Uses the 1981 PAS, the Tennessee Self Concept Scale, the Personality Research Form—Form E, the Hogan Empathy Scale, the Fundamental Interpersonal Correlations Orientation—Behavior, (FIRO-B), and the IPAT Anxiety Scale Questionnaire.

Grossberg, John M.; Alf, Edward F. Interaction with pet dogs: Effects on human cardiovascular response. *Journal of the Delta Society,* 2(1) 1985 Winter:20–27.

Use the Jenkins Activity Survey and the 1981 PAS.

Hama, Haruyo; Yogo, Masao; Matsuyama, Yoshinori. Effects of stroking horses on both humans' and horses' heart rate responses. *Japanese Psychological Research,* 38(2) 1996 May:66–73.

Subjects were selected from Doshisha University male students on the basis of their responses to a Japanese language version of the 1981 PAS.

Herrald, Mary M.; Tomaka, Joe; Medina, Amanda Y. Pet ownership predicts adherence to cardiovascular rehabilitation. *Journal of Applied Social Psychology,* 32(6) 2002 Jun:1107–23.

Use measures of self-esteem (Rosenberg, 1965), personal efficacy (Spheres of Control Personal Efficacy Subscale; Paulhus, 1983), optimism (Life Orientation Test; Scheier & Carver, 1985), sense of coherence (Antonovsky, 1987), and a shortened version of perceived stress (Cohen, Kamarck & Mermelstein, 1983). The questionnaire includes the NEO Five Factor Personality Inventory (Costa & McCrae, 1985), including its subscale that measures activity level; the fitness and health subscale of the Multidimensional Body-Self Relations Questionnaire (Cash, 1990), a modified version of the Interpersonal Support Evaluation List (Cohen & Hoberman, 1983), and the Sickness Impact Profile (Bergner, Bobbitt, Carter & Gilson, 1981). The Pet Attitude Scale used is a shortened, four-item version. All use a five-point scale ranging from 0 (disagree strongly) to 4 (agree strongly).

Jenkins, Judy L. Psychological effects of petting a companion animal. *Psychological Reports,* 58(1) 1986 Feb:21–22.

Uses the 1981 PAS to screen all subjects for positive regard for pets.

Kelly, Theresa A. Pet facilitated therapy in an outpatient setting. 2001. iii, 97 leaves. Unpublished Psy.D. thesis, University of Northern Colorado, 2001. Not seen. Abstract in *Dissertation Abstracts International,* Section B: The Sciences & Engineering, 62(9-B) 2002 Mar:4222-B.

Uses the 1981 PAS, the Symptom Checklist-90-R (SCL-90-R), and the Client Satisfaction Questionnaire (CSQ).

Lago, Dan J.; Kafer, Rudy; Delaney, Mary; Connell, Cathleen M. Assessment of favorable attitudes toward pets: Development and preliminary validation of self-report pet relationship scales. *Anthrozoös,* 1(4) 1988 Spring:240–54.

Validation studies of the Pet Relationship Scale were based on comparison with the 1981 PAS.

Miura, A.; Bradshaw, J. W. S.; Tanida, H. Childhood experiences and attitudes towards animal issues: A comparison of young adults in Japan and the UK. *Animal Welfare,* 11(4) 2002:437–48.

The 1981 PAS is included in a questionnaire of 47 questions, translated into Japanese and then back-translated, to check for retention of meaning.

Moroi, Katsuhide. Loneliness and attitudes toward pets. *Jikken Shakai Shinrigaku Kenkyu = Japanese Journal of Experimental Social Psychology,* 24(1) 1984:93–103.

Text in Japanese with English abstract. Uses the UCLA Loneliness Scale, the 1981 PAS, and the College Life Questionnaire.

Panzer-Koplow, Sheridan Lynn. Effects of animal-assisted therapy on depression and moral among nursing home residents. 2000. vi, 99 leaves: illus. Unpublished Ed.D. thesis, Rutgers, the State University of New Jersey-New Brunswick, Graduate School of Education, 2000. Not seen. Abstract in *Dissertation Abstracts International,* Section B: The Sciences & Engineering, 61(1-B) 2000 Jul:544-B.

Uses the Beck Depression Inventory II, the Geriatric Depression Scale, the PGC Morale Scale, and the 1981 PAS.

Paul, E. S.; Serpell, J. A. Childhood pet keeping and humane attitudes in young adulthood. *Animal Welfare,* 2(4) 1993:321–37.

Use the 1981 PAS, an anglicized Scale of Attitudes towards the Treatment of Animals (Bowd), and the Empathy Scale (Mehrabian & Epstein, 1972).

Planchon, Lynn A.; Templer, Donald I. The correlates of grief after death of a pet. *Anthrozoös,* 9(2–3) 1996:107–13.

Use the 1981 PAS and the Death Depression Scale.

Planchon, Lynn A., Templer, Donald I.; Stokes, Shelley; Keller, Jacqueline. Death of a companion cat or dog and human bereavement: Psychosocial variables. *Society & Animals,* 10(1) 2002:93–105.

Use the Beck Depression Inventory, the CENSHARE Pet Attachment Survey, the Death Depression Scale, the 1981 PAS, and the Pet Loss Questionnaire.

This article is available at the website www.psyeta.org/sa/sa10.1/planchon.shtml (accessed October 15, 2003).

Poresky, Robert H.; Hendrix, Charles; Mosier, Jacob E.; Samuelson, Marvin L. The Companion Animal Bonding Scale: Internal reliability and construct validity. *Psychological Reports,* 60(3, Pt.1) 1987 Jun:743–46.

Construct validity of CABS was indicated "by significant correlations between scores on the [1981] Pet Attitude Scale and the childhood and contemporary bonding scale. . . ."

Ruckdeschel, Katy; Van Haitsma, Kimberley. The impact of live-in animals and plants on nursing home residents: A pilot longitudinal intervention. *Alzheimer's Care Quarterly: ACQ,* 2(4) 2001 Fall:17–27.

Use the 1981 PAS, Quality of Life in Dementia Scale, Pearline and Schooler's Mastery Scale, UCLA Loneliness Scale, and Lawton's Apparent Affect Rating Scale.

Schenk, Suzanne Ashley; Templer, Donald I.; Peters, Noel B.; Schmidt, Mari. The genesis and correlates of attitudes toward pets. *Anthrozoös,* 7(1) 1994:60–68.

Use the 1981 PAS and the Family Environment Scale (Moos, 1974).

Straede, Cheryl M.; Gates, G. Richard. Psychological health in a population of Australian cat owners. *Anthrozoös,* 6(1) 1993:30–42.

Use the 1981 PAS, Sleep Disturbance Questionnaire, Nurturance Questionnaire, General Health Questionnaire (CHQ-30), Beck Depression Inventory, Marlowe-Crowne Social Desirability Scale, State-Trait Anxiety Inventory, and Life Events Inventory.

Vormbrock, Julia K.; Grossberg, John M. Cardiovascular effects of human-pet interactions. *Journal of Behavioral Medicine,* 11(5) 1988:509–17.

Use a modified version of the 1981 PAS, and subjects' ratings of their liking for pet dogs (positive or neutral). Items 1–10, 13, 15, 16 and 18 (a total of 14) were rephrased to refer specifically to pet dogs, an identical set added to refer to pet cats, and an additional set to refer to pet reptiles. An additional scale asked subjects to rate their liking of dogs, cats, and reptiles, ranging from "I love them" to "I hate them."

Notes:

Reverse score items 4, 6, 9, 12, 13, and 17 (e.g., if the subject uses 7, change it to 1; if the subject uses 6, change it to 2, etc.) and total them. Sum the remaining 18 item responses to obtain total scale scores. Add the two totals together; that is the subject's pet attitude score. Scores can range from 18 to 126. The higher the score, the more positive the person's feelings are toward pets.

Also cited in the Educational Testing Service, ETS Test Collection Service website, www.ets.org/test-coll/ (Revised October 3, 2003; accessed May 18, 2004). The alternative website is http://sydneyplus.ets.org/ (accessed October 23, 2004).

This measure is also available from the Behavioral Measurement Database Services, producer of the database Health and Psychosocial Instruments (HaPI), phone 412/687-6850, fax 412/687-5213 or email: bmdshapi@aol.com for ordering information. Provide the BMDS accession number, 13718, and the title, Pet Attitude Scale.

The 1981 PAS is also available in William Langston, *Research methods laboratory manual for psychology* (Pacific Grove, CA: Wadsworth Group, 2002), chapter 3, supplement 1, page 33.

Copyright Notice:

Pet Attitude Scale—Modified

Please answer each of the following questions as honestly as you can, in terms of how you feel right now. This questionnaire is anonymous and no one will ever know which answers are yours. So, don't worry about how you think others might answer these questions. There aren't any right or wrong answers. All that matters is that you express your true thoughts on the subject.

Please answer by circling one of the following seven numbers for each question.

1	2	3	4	5	6	7
Strongly Disagree	Moderately Disagree	Slightly Disagree	Unsure	Slightly Agree	Moderately Agree	Strongly Agree

For example, if you slightly disagree with the first item, you would circle the number three for slightly disagree.

---

1. I really like seeing pets enjoy their food.

1	2	3	4	5	6	7
Strongly Disagree	Moderately Disagree	Slightly Disagree	Unsure	Slightly Agree	Moderately Agree	Strongly Agree

2. My pet means more to me than any of my friends (or would if I had one).

1	2	3	4	5	6	7
Strongly Disagree	Moderately Disagree	Slightly Disagree	Unsure	Slightly Agree	Moderately Agree	Strongly Agree

3. I would like to have a pet in my home.

1	2	3	4	5	6	7
Strongly Disagree	Moderately Disagree	Slightly Disagree	Unsure	Slightly Agree	Moderately Agree	Strongly Agree

4. Having pets is a waste of money.

1	2	3	4	5	6	7
Strongly Disagree	Moderately Disagree	Slightly Disagree	Unsure	Slightly Agree	Moderately Agree	Strongly Agree

5. House pets add happiness to my life (or would if I had one).

1	2	3	4	5	6	7
Strongly Disagree	Moderately Disagree	Slightly Disagree	Unsure	Slightly Agree	Moderately Agree	Strongly Agree

6. I feel that pets should always be kept outside.

1	2	3	4	5	6	7
Strongly Disagree	Moderately Disagree	Slightly Disagree	Unsure	Slightly Agree	Moderately Agree	Strongly Agree

7. I spend time every day playing with my pet (or would if I had one).

1	2	3	4	5	6	7
Strongly Disagree	Moderately Disagree	Slightly Disagree	Unsure	Slightly Agree	Moderately Agree	Strongly Agree

8. I have occasionally communicated with my pet and understood what it was trying to express (or would if I had one).

1	2	3	4	5	6	7
Strongly Disagree	Moderately Disagree	Slightly Disagree	Unsure	Slightly Agree	Moderately Agree	Strongly Agree

9. The world would be a better place if people would stop spending so much time caring for their pets and started caring more for other human beings instead.

1	2	3	4	5	6	7
Strongly Disagree	Moderately Disagree	Slightly Disagree	Unsure	Slightly Agree	Moderately Agree	Strongly Agree

10. I like to feed animals out of my hand.

1	2	3	4	5	6	7
Strongly Disagree	Moderately Disagree	Slightly Disagree	Unsure	Slightly Agree	Moderately Agree	Strongly Agree

11. I love pets.

1	2	3	4	5	6	7
Strongly Disagree	Moderately Disagree	Slightly Disagree	Unsure	Slightly Agree	Moderately Agree	Strongly Agree

12. Animals belong in the wild or in zoos, but not in the home.

1	2	3	4	5	6	7
Strongly Disagree	Moderately Disagree	Slightly Disagree	Unsure	Slightly Agree	Moderately Agree	Strongly Agree

13. If you keep pets in the house you can expect a lot of damage to furniture.

1	2	3	4	5	6	7
Strongly Disagree	Moderately Disagree	Slightly Disagree	Unsure	Slightly Agree	Moderately Agree	Strongly Agree

14. I like house pets.

1	2	3	4	5	6	7
Strongly Disagree	Moderately Disagree	Slightly Disagree	Unsure	Slightly Agree	Moderately Agree	Strongly Agree

15. Pets are fun but it's not worth the trouble of owning one.

1	2	3	4	5	6	7
Strongly Disagree	Moderately Disagree	Slightly Disagree	Unsure	Slightly Agree	Moderately Agree	Strongly Agree

16. I frequently talk to my pets (or would if I had one).

1	2	3	4	5	6	7
Strongly Disagree	Moderately Disagree	Slightly Disagree	Unsure	Slightly Agree	Moderately Agree	Strongly Agree

17. I hate animals.

1	2	3	4	5	6	7
Strongly Disagree	Moderately Disagree	Slightly Disagree	Unsure	Slightly Agree	Moderately Agree	Strongly Agree

18. You should treat your house pets with as much respect as you would a human member of your family.

1	2	3	4	5	6	7
Strongly Disagree	Moderately Disagree	Slightly Disagree	Unsure	Slightly Agree	Moderately Agree	Strongly Agree

Pet Bonding Scale, PBS
(Angle, Blumentritt, Swank, 1993)

Developed in:

Angle, Rebecca L. Utilization of the Pet Bonding Scale to examine the relation between the human/companion animal bond and self-esteem in pre-adolescence. 1994. xii, [3], 57 leaves. Unpublished Ph.D. thesis, University of Houston, College of Education, 1994. Adviser: John P. Gaa. Not seen. Abstract in *Dissertation Abstracts International,* Section B: Sciences & Engineering, 55(10-B) 1995 Apr:4618-B. The scale appears on pages 43–45 of the dissertation.

Also uses a demographic questionnaire and the Self-Description Questionnaire-1 (SDA-1, March, 1987).

Used in:

Bierer, Robert Elias. The relationship between pet bonding, self-esteem, and empathy in pre-adolescents. 2000. xiv, 138 leaves: 1 col. illus. Unpublished Ph.D. thesis, University of New Mexico, 2000. Not seen. Abstract in *Dissertation Abstracts International,* Section B: Sciences & Engineering, 61(11-B) 2001 May:6183-B.

Also uses the Coopersmith Self-Esteem Inventory and the Boat Index of Empathy for Children and Adolescents. The PBS was modified and used only with dog owners.

Sezov, Deborah D. The contribution of empathy to harmony in interpersonal relationships. 2002. ix, 372 leaves: Forms. Unpublished Ph.D. thesis, Temple University, 2002. Not seen. Abstract in *Dissertation Abstracts International,* Section B: Sciences & Engineering, 63(6-B) 2002 Dec:3046-B.

Uses the PBS and the Empathy Measure for Preschoolers (EMP).

"Scores on the Pet Bonding Scale (PBS) were not predictive of empathy or of quality of interaction with a live rabbit. However, the quality of interaction with the rabbit, pet ownership, and length of pet ownership were positively related to empathy. The Pet Bonding Scale appears to be susceptible to social desirability and halo effect confounding in part due to lack of camouflaging the intent of the questions" (from the abstract).

Pet Bonding Scale

Answer these questions only about the pet you named as closest to being your friend.

1. My pet can make me laugh.   Never_____   Usually_____   Always_____

2. I have a lot of fun with my pet.   Never_____   Usually_____   Always_____

3. My pet makes me feel important.   Never_____   Usually_____   Always_____

4. I have warm feelings when I think about my pet.   Never_____   Usually_____   Always_____

5. I like to spend a lot of time with my pet.   Never_____   Usually_____   Always_____

6. My pet loves me.   Never_____   Usually_____   Always_____

7. My pet misses me when I am gone.   Never_____   Usually_____   Always_____

8. I like to talk to my pet about things that are   Never_____   Usually_____   Always_____
    important to me.

9. I like to talk to my pet.   Never_____   Usually_____   Always_____

10. My pet understands my feelings.   Never_____   Usually_____   Always_____

11. I can tell secrets to my pet.   Never_____   Usually_____   Always_____

12. Sometimes my only friend is my pet.   Never_____   Usually_____   Always_____

13. My pet loves me no matter what.   Never_____   Usually_____   Always_____

14. One of my favorite things to do is spend time   Never_____   Usually_____   Always_____
    with my pet.

15. My pet is an important part of my family.   Never_____   Usually_____   Always_____

16. My pet understands what I say.   Never_____   Usually_____   Always_____

17. I would be very upset if something happened to   Never_____   Usually_____   Always_____
    my pet.

18. I try to protect my pet. Never_____ Usually_____ Always_____

19. I keep pictures of my pet. Never_____ Usually_____ Always_____

20. My pet stays close to me when I am upset. Never_____ Usually_____ Always_____

21. My pet has feelings. Never_____ Usually_____ Always_____

22. I think about my pet when we are not together. Never_____ Usually_____ Always_____

23. I miss my pet when I am gone. Never_____ Usually_____ Always_____

24. My pet is important to me. Never_____ Usually_____ Always_____

25. I am proud of my pet. Never_____ Usually_____ Always_____

Pet Expectations Inventory

(George, 1992)

also known as George's Pet Expectations Inventory

Developed for and published in:

Kidd, Aline H.; Kidd, Robert M.; George, Carol C. Veterinarians and successful pet adoptions. *Psychological Reports,* 71 1992:551–7.

The Pet Expectations Inventory is published on pages 556–57.

Used in:

Kidd, Aline H.; Kidd, Robert M.; George, Carol C. Successful and unsuccessful pet adoptions. *Psychological Reports,* 70 1992:547–61.

Pet Expectations Inventory

Type of pet being adopted: CAT   DOG   OTHER   Specify _____

CHILDREN (list by sex and age only):

PETS PRESENTLY OWNED (if any):

DOG(S) _____ How long owned? _____   CAT(S) _____ How long owned? _____

I. Please answer the following questions about the role you expect the pet to take in your life by circling the appropriate number below the question. Please complete all items. Do not leave questions unanswered.

	Strongly Agree						Strongly Disagree
A. I expect the pet to be a companion for me.	7	6	5	4	3	2	1
B. I expect the pet always to be there for me.	7	6	5	4	3	2	1
C. I expect to talk to my pet.	7	6	5	4	3	2	1
D. I expect my pet to make me feel better when I am sad or discouraged.	7	6	5	4	3	2	1
E. I expect to stroke and cuddle my pet.	7	6	5	4	3	2	1
F. I expect my pet to love me.	7	6	5	4	3	2	1
G. I expect my pet to be a source of laughter.	7	6	5	4	3	2	1
H. I expect my pet to be an interesting topic of conversation with friends and relatives.	7	6	5	4	3	2	1
I. I expect to play with my pet.	7	6	5	4	3	2	1
J. I expect my pet to protect me.	7	6	5	4	3	2	1
K. I expect to teach my pet tricks.	7	6	5	4	3	2	1
L. I expect to confide in my pet.	7	6	5	4	3	2	1
M. I expect my pet to be a living thing for me to love.	7	6	5	4	3	2	1

II. If you have children, please answer the following questions about the role you expect the pet to take in your child's development by circling the appropriate number below the question. Please read each question carefully, and complete all items. Do not leave questions unanswered.

	Strongly Agree						Strongly Disagree
A. I expect the pet to be a companion for my child.	7	6	5	4	3	2	1
B. I expect the pet to keep my child busy so I can work or relax.	7	6	5	4	3	2	1
C. I expect the pet to help my child learn to be sensitive to others.	7	6	5	4	3	2	1
D. I expect the pet to be my child's playmate.	7	6	5	4	3	2	1
E. I expect my pet to help my child learn to take responsibility.	7	6	5	4	3	2	1
F. I expect my child to feed the pet.	7	6	5	4	3	2	1
G. I expect my child to exercise the pet.	7	6	5	4	3	2	1
H. I expect my child to discipline the pet.	7	6	5	4	3	2	1
I. I expect the pet to provide emotional comfort for my child.	7	6	5	4	3	2	1
J. I expect the pet to help my child to be more affectionate.	7	6	5	4	3	2	1
K. I expect my child to care for the pet (e.g., clean litter box).	7	6	5	4	3	2	1
L. I expect the pet to sleep with my child. (Omit if pet is not a pet that can sleep with your child.)	7	6	5	4	3	2	1
M. I expect the pet to occupy my child so he/she will not fight with brothers or sisters.	7	6	5	4	3	2	1
N. I expect my child to cuddle or show affection to the pet.	7	6	5	4	3	2	1
O. I expect to remind my child daily to care for the pet.	7	6	5	4	3	2	1
P. I expect the pet to protect my child.	7	6	5	4	3	2	1
Q. I expect the pet to provide physical comfort for my child.	7	6	5	4	3	2	1

Pet Friendship Scale, PFS

(Davis, 1995)

Published in:

Davis, Janet Haggerty; Juhasz, Anne McCreary. The preadolescent/pet friendship bond. *Anthrozoös,* 8(2) 1995:78–82.

"Pet Friendship Scale Responses," including the 26 statements, appear in Table 1, page 80.

The PFS is developed by modifying the Pet/Friend Q-Sort (PFQ), which Davis used in her thesis, The role of the family dog in the preadolescent's psychosocial development relative to selected dimensions of the self-concept, sex, and age (unpublished Ph.D. thesis, Loyola University of Chicago, 1987) and in her article Preadolescent self-concept development and pet ownership, *Anthrozoös,* 1(2) 1987 Fall:90–94.

The PFQ consists of 60 positive affective statements. The statements are based on research findings related to the emotional relationship of children and pets, interviews with preadolescents concerning their feelings about the family dog, and questionnaires used to identify attitudes toward pet ownership, including the Pet Attitude Scale (Templer et al., 1981). Twenty-three statements are taken from the PFQ, one from the PFQ is modified, and two were written for the PFS.

Pet Friendship Scale

How much are these statements like you and the family pet?

		Exactly like	Very much like	Pretty much like	Little bit like	Not like
1.	I can be myself with you.	1	2	3	4	5
2.	I like playing with you.	1	2	3	4	5
3.	I help you feel better if people are mad.	1	2	3	4	5
4.	I go to you when I'm bored.	1	2	3	4	5
5.	I feel sorry for you.	1	2	3	4	5
6.	I worry about you.	1	2	3	4	5
7.	I know what you want.	1	2	3	4	5
8.	I make you feel happy.	1	2	3	4	5
9.	I help you feel less lonely.	1	2	3	4	5
10.	I think you are funny.	1	2	3	4	5
11.	I make you feel safe.	1	2	3	4	5
12.	I like spending time with you.	1	2	3	4	5
13.	I go to you when I'm lonely.	1	2	3	4	5
14.	I love you.	1	2	3	4	5
15.	I can act crazy with you.	1	2	3	4	5
16.	I think you are smart.	1	2	3	4	5
17.	I make you feel liked.	1	2	3	4	5
		Exactly like	Very much like	Pretty much like	Little bit like	Not like

	Exactly like	Very much like	Pretty much like	Little bit like	Not like
18. I like you the way you are.	1	2	3	4	5
19. I help you feel less sad.	1	2	3	4	5
20. I feel warm towards you.	1	2	3	4	5
21. I miss you when we are apart.	1	2	3	4	5
22. I protect you.	1	2	3	4	5
23. I take care of you.	1	2	3	4	5
24. I make you feel loved.	1	2	3	4	5
25. I think you are interesting.	1	2	3	4	5
26. I know what you need.	1	2	3	4	5
	Exactly like	Very much like	Pretty much like	Little bit like	Not like

Pet Relationship Scale, PRS

(Kafer, Lago, Wamboldt, Harrington, 1992)

The best source of information on this scale is found on Dan Lago's faculty website, www.personal.psu. edu/faculty/d/j/djl/research.htm. Under the Attitudes toward Animals: Scales for Empirical Research, there are three links to the broad set of 17 scales (116 items), carefully translated and back-translated into both French and Spanish, along with the English version. The three Pet Relationship Scales are subscales 14–16 of the Animal Relationship Scales.

Described & reported in:

Kafer, Rudy; Lago, Dan; Wamboldt, Patricia; Harrington, Fred. The Pet Relationship Scale: Replication of psychometric properties in random samples and association with attitudes toward wild animals. *Anthrozoös,* 5(2) 1992:93–105.

> Table 2, "Factor Structure of Pet Relationship Scales (random sample, Nova Scotia, N=1451)," page 98, and Table 3, "Pet Relationship Scale, Subscale Structure and Reliability (Nova Scotia, random sample, N=1451)," page 99.

Developed in:

Lago, Dan; Kafer, Rudy; Delaney, Mary; Connell, Cathleen. Assessment of favorable attitudes toward pets: Development and preliminary validation of self-report pet relationship scales. *Anthrozoös,* 1(4) 1988 Spring:240–54.

> Describe development of the PRS along with preliminary reliability and validity information. Validation studies were based on comparison of the PRS with the Pet Attitude Scale (Templer et al., 1981).

Used in the following studies of PACT, the People and Animals Coming Together program:

Connell, Cathleen M.; Lago, Daniel J. Favorable attitudes toward pets and happiness among the elderly, pages 241–50, in: Anderson, Robert K.; Hart, Benjamin L.; Hart, Lynette A. (editors). *The pet connection: Its influence on our health and quality of life.* Minneapolis, MN: Center to Study Human-Animal Relationships and Environments, University of Minnesota,1984.

Lago, Dan; Connell, Cathleen M.; Knight, Barbara. A companion animal program, pages 65–84, in: Smyer, Michael A.; Gatz, Margaret (editors). *Mental health and aging: Programs and evaluations.* (Sage studies in community mental health; vol. 8). Beverly Hills, CA: Sage Publications, 1983.

Lago, Daniel J.; Connell, Cathleen M.; Knight, Barbara. The effects of animal companionship on older persons living at home, pages 34–46, in: *The human-pet relationship:* International Symposium on the Occasion of the 80th Birthday of Nobel Prize Winner Prof. DDr. Konrad Lorenz held on October 27 and 28, 1983, in Vienna, Austria: Proceedings. Vienna: Institute of Interdisciplinary Research on the Human-Pet Relationship, 1985.

Lago, Dan; Delaney, Mary; Miller, Melody; Grill, Claire. Companion animals, attitudes toward pets, and health outcomes among the elderly: A long-term followup. *Anthrozoös,* 3(1) 1989 Summer:25–34.

Lago, Dan J.; Knight, Barbara; Connell, Cathleen. Relationships with companion animals among the rural elderly, pages [328]–340, in: Katcher, Aaron Honori; Beck, Alan M. (editors). *New perspectives on our life with companion animals.* Philadelphia: University of Pennsylvania Press, 1983.

Lago, Dan; Knight, Barbara; Rohrer-Dann, Mary; Friend, George. *The PACT manual: Promoting bonded relationships between people and animals.* University Park: Pennsylvania State University Press, 1985.

The PRS appears in appendix E, page 102.

Lago, Dan; Kotch-Jantzer, Catherine. Euthanasia of pet animals and the death of elderly owners: Implications for support of community-dwelling elderly pet owners, pages 148–156, in: Kay, William J.; Cohen, Susan P.; Nieburg, Herbert A.; Fudin, Carole E.; Grey, Ross E.; Kutscher, Austin H.; Osman, Mohamed M. (editors). *Euthanasia of the companion animal: The impact on pet owners, veterinarians, and society.* Philadelphia: Charles Press, 1988.

Used in:

Chumley, Perry R.; Gorski, June D.; Saxton, Arnold M.; Granger, Ben P.; New, John C., Jr. Companion animal attachment and military transfer. *Anthrozoös,* 6(4) 1993:258–73.

Combined PRS 1 and 2 (less item 10) and seven items from the Pet Attitude Scale (Templer et al., 1981) to form a 21-item Pet Attachment Survey with a 6-point Likert scale. This "Survey for Military Companion Animal Owners" (i.e., Pet Attachment Survey) is published on pages 272–73.

Holt, Margaret Lee. Effect of a pet dog on hypertensive process and self-disclosure during marital dialogue. 1995. ii, 206 leaves: illus. Unpublished Ed.D. thesis, Counseling Psychology Program, University of San Francisco, 1995. Abstract in *Dissertation Abstracts International,* Section B: The Sciences & Engineering, 56(8-B) 1996 Feb:4629-B.

Uses the PRS, the Modified Self-Disclosure (Chelune, 1976) and a short, modified form of the Human-Dog Interaction (Messent, 1983) coding systems.

Johnson, Rebecca A.; Meadows, Richard L. Older Latinos, pets, and health. *Western Journal of Nursing Research,* 24(6) 2002 Oct:609–20.

Use the Demographic Questionnaire (DQ), the PRS, twenty items from the Pet Attitude Inventory (PAI), the Iowa Self Assessment Inventory (ISAI), and the Self-Perceived Health Questionnaire.

Miller, Melody; Lago, Dan. Observed pet-owner in-home interactions: Species differences and association with the Pet Relationship Scale. *Anthrozoös,* 4(1) 1990 Summer:49–54.

Miller, Melody; Lago, Dan. The well-being of older women: The importance of pet and human relations. *Anthrozoös,* 3(4) 1990 Spring:245–48.

Use the PRS, a network resource mapping technique to identify people in social support, where the pet fits in this network, network interactions, and the Social Support Appraisal Scale (Vaux et al., 1986).

Norris, Patricia Ann Castle. Retirement, life satisfaction, and pet ownership: Please don't take my sunshine away. 1998. xiii, 162 leaves. Unpublished Ph.D. thesis in Leisure Studies, University of Illinois at Urbana-Champaign, 1998. Not seen. Abstract in *Dissertation Abstracts International,* Section A: The Humanities & Social Sciences, 59(9-A) 1999 Mar:3645-A.

Norris's questionnaire is based on the Satisfaction with Life Scale (Diener, 1994), the Involvement with Pets Scale (Norris, 1995), the PRS, and the Miller-Rada Commitment to Pets Scale (Staats et al., 1996). The entire questionnaire is reproduced in Appendix B, pages 139–45.

Zasloff, R. Lee; Kidd, Aline H. Loneliness and pet ownership among single women. *Psychological Reports,* 75 1994:747–52.

Use the PRS and the Pet Attitude Scale (Templer et al., 1981).

Notes:

A four-point Likert scale may be used, but will likely produce lower item-to-total correlations. We do not recommend a scale with a neutral point.

Copyright Notice:

Pet Relationship Scales

Instructions:

Please answer every question. There are no right or wrong answers. We simply seek your honest opinion of how much you agree or disagree with each statement.

Pet Relationship Scale 1 Items
(Affectionate companionship)

1. There are times I'd be lonely except for my pet.

1	2	3	4	5	6
Strongly Disagree	Moderately Disagree	Mildly Disagree	Mildly Agree	Moderately Agree	Strongly Agree

2. My pet and I watch TV together frequently.

1	2	3	4	5	6
Strongly Disagree	Moderately Disagree	Mildly Disagree	Mildly Agree	Moderately Agree	Strongly Agree

3. I give gifts to my pet for birthdays and special occasions.

1	2	3	4	5	6
Strongly Disagree	Moderately Disagree	Mildly Disagree	Mildly Agree	Moderately Agree	Strongly Agree

4. My pet is a valuable possession.

1	2	3	4	5	6
Strongly Disagree	Moderately Disagree	Mildly Disagree	Mildly Agree	Moderately Agree	Strongly Agree

5. I talk to my pet about things that bother me.

1	2	3	4	5	6
Strongly Disagree	Moderately Disagree	Mildly Disagree	Mildly Agree	Moderately Agree	Strongly Agree

6. Making me laugh is part of my pet's job.

1	2	3	4	5	6
Strongly Disagree	Moderately Disagree	Mildly Disagree	Mildly Agree	Moderately Agree	Strongly Agree

7. I miss my pet when I am away.

1	2	3	4	5	6
Strongly Disagree	Moderately Disagree	Mildly Disagree	Mildly Agree	Moderately Agree	Strongly Agree

8. My pet gives me reason for getting up in the morning.

1	2	3	4	5	6
Strongly Disagree	Moderately Disagree	Mildly Disagree	Mildly Agree	Moderately Agree	Strongly Agree

Pet Relationship Scale 2 Items
(Equal Family Member)

9. My pet is a member of the family.

1	2	3	4	5	6
Strongly Disagree	Moderately Disagree	Mildly Disagree	Mildly Agree	Moderately Agree	Strongly Agree

10. I share my food with my pet.

1	2	3	4	5	6
Strongly Disagree	Moderately Disagree	Mildly Disagree	Mildly Agree	Moderately Agree	Strongly Agree

11. My pet knows when I'm upset and tries to comfort me.

1	2	3	4	5	6
Strongly Disagree	Moderately Disagree	Mildly Disagree	Mildly Agree	Moderately Agree	Strongly Agree

12. My pet is constantly at my side.

1	2	3	4	5	6
Strongly Disagree	Moderately Disagree	Mildly Disagree	Mildly Agree	Moderately Agree	Strongly Agree

13. My pet is an equal in this family.

1	2	3	4	5	6
Strongly Disagree	Moderately Disagree	Mildly Disagree	Mildly Agree	Moderately Agree	Strongly Agree

14. I treat my pet to anything I happen to be eating if he/she seems interested.

1	2	3	4	5	6
Strongly Disagree	Moderately Disagree	Mildly Disagree	Mildly Agree	Moderately Agree	Strongly Agree

15. In many ways my pet is the best friend I have.

1	2	3	4	5	6
Strongly Disagree	Moderately Disagree	Mildly Disagree	Mildly Agree	Moderately Agree	Strongly Agree

Pet Relationship Scale 3 Items
(Mutual Physical Activity)

16. My pet helps me to be more physically active.

1	2	3	4	5	6
Strongly Disagree	Moderately Disagree	Mildly Disagree	Mildly Agree	Moderately Agree	Strongly Agree

17. I spend a lot of time cleaning and grooming my pet.

1	2	3	4	5	6
Strongly Disagree	Moderately Disagree	Mildly Disagree	Mildly Agree	Moderately Agree	Strongly Agree

18. I take my pet along when I go jogging or walking.

1	2	3	4	5	6
Strongly Disagree	Moderately Disagree	Mildly Disagree	Mildly Agree	Moderately Agree	Strongly Agree

19. My pet goes to the veterinarian for regular checkups and shots.

1	2	3	4	5	6
Strongly Disagree	Moderately Disagree	Mildly Disagree	Mildly Agree	Moderately Agree	Strongly Agree

20. I enjoy having my pet ride in the car with me.

1	2	3	4	5	6
Strongly Disagree	Moderately Disagree	Mildly Disagree	Mildly Agree	Moderately Agree	Strongly Agree

21. I bathe my pet regularly.

1	2	3	4	5	6
Strongly Disagree	Moderately Disagree	Mildly Disagree	Mildly Agree	Moderately Agree	Strongly Agree

22. My pet and I often take walks together.

1	2	3	4	5	6
Strongly Disagree	Moderately Disagree	Mildly Disagree	Mildly Agree	Moderately Agree	Strongly Agree

Index & Annotated Bibliography of Related Measures

1. Animal-Assisted Therapy Evaluation Instrument

Reported and used in:

Velde, Sarah. The development and validation of a research evaluation instrument to assess the effectiveness of animal-assisted therapy. 2005. [vii], 202 leaves. Unpublished Ph.D. thesis in Health Administration, Kennedy-Western University, 2005.

> The final version of the AAT tool consists of Appendix L, Template for Guiding & Evaluation Animal-Assisted Therapy, pages.198–202.

> This thesis is available through the Delta Society website, at www.deltasociety.org/AnimalsResourcesResources.htm# (accessed 23 Apr 2006).

2. Animal-Assisted Therapy: Therapy Effectiveness Evaluation

Reported in:

Lawrence, Marilyn. Animal-assisted therapy: Therapy effectiveness evaluation. (Rev. ed.) [Fort Myers, FL]: M.K. Lawrence, 2002, 2004. one compact disc (4¾ inches) of 44 pages (mostly forms)

> Contents: Overview — Objectives — Client assessment — Therapy session documentation — Therapy session summary — Document samples.

> Contact: Marilyn K Lawrence, 16031 South Pebble Lane, Fort Myers, Florida 33912 USA; email: mklaw@earthlink.net.

Reported and used in:

Glacken, Joan; Lawrence, Marilyn K. Content validation, and pilot studies of the Therapy Effectiveness Evaluation for Animal-Assisted Therapy instrument. *American Journal of Recreation Therapy,* 4(3) 2005 Summer:21–24.

3. Animal Empathy Scale, AES (Paul, 2000)

Reported and used in:

Paul, Elizabeth S. Empathy with animals and with humans: Are they linked? *Anthrozoös,* 13(4) 2000:194–202.

> Appendix I, The [22-item] Animal Empathy Scale, appears on page 202.

The 28-item scale is used in:

Paul, E. S.; Podberscek, A. L. Veterinary education and students' attitudes towards animal welfare. *Veterinary Record,* 146 2000:269–72.

Also used by:

Taylor, Heidi; Williams, Pauline; Gray, David. Homelessness and dog ownership: An investigation into animal empathy, attachment, crime, drug use, health and public opinion. *Anthrozoös,* 17(4) 2004: 353–68.

> Adapted AES, using only ten statements selected for their relevance to both securely housed and homeless populations. Also adapted the Companion Animal Bonding Scale (CABS; Poresky et al., 1987), using eight questions only, of which the wording of two was changed. "Summary of Questions Used in the Study" appears as Table 1, page 358.

4. Animal Fears Questionnaire (Davey, 1994)

Reported in:

Davey, Graham C. L. Self-reported fears to common indigenous animals in an adult UK population: The role of disgust sensitivity, *British Journal of Psychology,* 85(4) 1994 Nov:541–54.

Used by:

Arrindell, Willem Alexander. Phobic dimensions: IV. The structure of animal fears. *Behaviour Research and Therapy,* 28(5) 2000 May:509–30.

   Modifies both the methodology and the Animal Fears Questionnaire.

5. Animal Human Compatibility Scale (Budge, Jones, Spicer, 1997)

Reported in:

Budge, R. C.; Jones, B.; Spicer, J. A procedure for assessing human-companion animal compatibility, pages 82–6, in: *Proceedings of the First International Conference on Veterinary Behavioural Medicine,* Birmingham, UK, April 1 & 2, 1997; Editors: D. S. Mills, S. E. Heath, L. J. Harrington (Potters Bar, England: Universities Federation for Animal Welfare, 1997).

   This measure is not reproduced in this contribution or in the article cited below.

Used by:

Budge, R. Claire; Spicer, John; Jones, Boyd; St. George, Ross. Health correlates of compatibility and attachment in human-companion animal relationships. *Society & Animals,* 6(3) 1998:219–34.

   "The version used . . . consists of two subscales, Pet Compatibility and Owner Compatibility, which contain 26 and 15 items respectively. For each item, an attribute of the pet and owner relationship is presented on a 10-point rating scale with opposite poles at either end. For example an item concerning the pet's playfulness presents a scale ranging from 'not at all playful' to 'very playful.' Participants were required to rate each item twice, once with respect to their actual pet or themselves as owners and a second time with respect to the ideal pet or owner. The absolute difference between the actual and ideal rating provided an index of their compatibility on that attribute. Scores were averaged across the Pet and Owner items respectively to produce two subscale scores and across all scores to produce an overall Compatibility index. It is important to note that because of the direction of the scoring, a higher score meant a less compatible relationship. The Pet and Owner subscales had Cronbach's alpha (Thorndike 1982) coefficients of .84 and .87 respectively, indicating an acceptable level of internal consistency. The subscales were moderately correlated (r=.49), suggesting that they were capturing similar aspects of pet-owner compatibility" (page 223).

6. Animal Preference Test, APT (Krevelen, 1955)

Reported in:

Krevelen, D. Arn van. The use of Pigem's Test with children. Journal of Projective Techniques, 20(2) 1956 Jun:235–42.

   In its original form, Pigem's Wishing Test consists of two questions: the first, "What would you like to be if you had to return to this world and you could not be a person? You may be whatever you like. Choose from everything that exists. What would you like to be?" the second, "Just imagine that I have never seen what you chose and that I know nothing about it. Describe to me what it is like." Krevelen asked children an additional question, "What would you like not to be?" and for their explanation.

Original reference:

Pigem, José M. La prueba de la expresión desiderativa. Barcelona: Libraria de Ciencias Médicas, 1949.

Used by:

Rojas, Evelyn Baez; Tuber, Steven. The Animal Preference Test and its relationship to behavioral problems in young children. Journal of Personality Assessment, 57(1) 1991:141–8.

    Also uses the Achenbach Child Behavior Checklist, CBCL.

Animal-Related Trauma Inventory

See the entry Boat Inventory on Animal-Related Experiences, BIARE (Boat 1998).

7. Animal Thematic Apperception Test, ATAT (Lockwood, 1983)

Lockwood, Randall. Influence of animals on social perception, pages 64–71, in: Katcher, Aaron H.; Beck, Alan M. (editors). *New perspectives on our lives with animal companions* (Philadelphia: University of Pennsylvania Press, 1983).

    The ATAT does not appear in this contribution. It uses five ambiguous scenes containing people and animals, and five identical scenes without animals, to assess subjects' attitudes toward animals, i.e., dogs and urban pigeons. It also uses one set of semantic differential scales for people, another set for the mood or tone of the scene (page 67). Used an additional Experience with Animals Questionnaire (pages 67–8).

    The scenes are modeled after those in Henry A. Murray and Staff of the Harvard Psychological Clinic, *Thematic apperception test manual* (Cambridge, Mass.: Harvard University Press, 1943). The TAT and analysis sheet are available in the Educational Testing Service database, at http://SydneyPlus.ets.org/database. TestCollection.

Validated in:

Friedmann, Erika; Lockwood, Randall. Validation and use of the Animal Thematic Apperception Test (ATAT). *Anthrozoös,* 4(3) 1991 Winter:174–83.

    Figures 1–3, pages 178–9, show the scenes with and without the animals present.

Friedmann, Erika; Locker, Barbra Zuck; Lockwood, Randall. Perception of animals and cardiovascular responses during verbalization with an animal present. *Anthrozoös,* 6(2) 1993:115–34.

    Figure 1, which consists of the individual scenes, appears on page 120.

8. Assessment of Dangerousness in Perpetrators of Animal Cruelty (Lockwood, 1998)

Available in:

Clinical assessment of juvenile animal cruelty (Lewchanin, Zimmerman, 2000). See entry in this bibliography.

Attachment to Pets Scale, APS

See the Lexington Attachment to Pets Scales, LAPS (Johnson, Garrity, Stallones, 1992), in the measures.

9. Attitude toward Animals and Attitude toward People Scales (Ray, 1982)

Reported in:

Ray, John J. Love of animals and love of people. *Journal of Social Psychology,* 116(2) 1982 Apr:299–300.

  Available from Dr. Ray at his website: http://jonjayray.tripod.com/attanim.html (accessed August 4, 2006).

Used by:

DeRosa, Bill. Extending humaneness from animals to people: A look at the transference theory. *Humane Education,* 1984 Jun:25.

Ojha, Hardeo. The relationship of authoritarianism to locus of control, love of animals and people, and reference for political ideology. *Psychological Studies,* 42(1) 1997 Mar:32–36.

St. Yves, A.; Freeston, M. H.; Jacques, C.; Robitaille, C. Love of animals and interpersonal affectionate behavior. *Psychological Reports,* 67(3 pt 2) 1990 Dec:1067–75.

Attitudes towards Dogs, DAQ

See the entry Dog Attitude Questionnaire, DAQ (Miura, Bradshaw, Tanida 2000).

10. Attitudes toward Responsible Pet Ownership (Selby et al., 1979)

Reported in:

Selby, Lloyd A.; Rhoades, John D.; Hewett, John E.; Irvin, James A. A survey of attitudes toward responsible pet ownership. *Public Health Reports,* 94(4) 1979 Jul-Aug:380–86.

  Items in the questionnaire are given in Table 2, "Reponses to Questionnaire Items Directly Related to Overpopulations of Dogs and Cats," pages 382–84. Subjects used a five-point Likert scale: strongly disagree via neutral to strongly agree.

Used by:

Selby, Lloyd A.; Rhoades, John D. Attitudes of the public towards dogs and cats as companion animals. *Journal of Small Animal Practice,* 22 1981:129–37.

  The items reported here cover 44 items related to the value of the dog as a companion animal, 51 items related to the value of the cat as a companion animal, and 18 items separately evaluated.

11. Battered Partner Shelter Survey, BPSS/Pet Maltreatment Survey (Ascione, Weber, 1995)

12. Battered Partner Shelter Survey, BPSS/Pet Maltreatment Survey. Mother/Child Version (Ascione, Weber, 1995)

Items 9 and 10 were prepared by Frank R. Ascione and Claudia Weber at the Department of Psychology, Utah State University.

Item 9 is also used by:

Ascione, Frank R.; Weber, Claudia V.; Wood, David S. Final Report on the Project entitled: Animal Welfare and Domestic Violence.

  Originally submitted to The Geraldine R. Dodge Foundation, April 25, 1997. See the website www.vachss.com/guest_dispatches/ascione_2.html (accessed July 4, 2003).

13. Boat Inventory on Animal-Related Experiences, BIARE (Boat, 1998)

Developed for:

Baker, Dewleen G.; Boat, Barbara W.; Grinvalsky, Henry T.; Geracioti, Thomas D., Jr. Interpersonal trauma and animal-related experiences in female and male military veterans: Implications for program development. *Military Medicine,* 163(1) 1998 Jan:20–6.

Published in:

Boat, Barbara W. Abuse of children and animals: Using the links to inform child assessment protection, pages 83–100, in: Ascione, Frank R.; Arkow, Phil (editors). *Child abuse, domestic violence and animal abuse: Linking the circles of compassion for prevention and intervention.* West Lafayette, Ind.: Purdue University Press, 1999.

"Appendix: Boat Inventory on Animal-Related Experiences," pages 94–100.

A semi-structured inventory to be used as a screening and information-gathering instrument, good for support in a clinical setting, less useful for community samples or for self-administering purposes, because it is lengthy. Not standardized or normed.

Used in:

Flynn, Clifton P. Animal abuse in childhood and later support for interpersonal violence in families. *Society & Animals,* 7(2) 1999:161–72.

Modifies the questionnaire developed by Miller and Knutson. The perpetuation of animal abuse was measured using five items from the BIARE.

Flynn, Clifton P. Exploring the link between corporal punishment and children's cruelty to animals. *Journal of Marriage & the Family,* 61(4) 1999 Nov:971–81.

Henry, Bill C. The relationship between animal cruelty, delinquency, and attitudes toward the treatment of animals. *Society & Animals,* 12(3) 2004:185–207.

Adapted the Flynn survey by deleting the section on sexual contact.

Miller, Karla S.; Knutson, John F. Reports of severe physical punishment and exposure to animal cruelty by inmates convicted of felonies and by university students. *Child Abuse and Neglect,* 21(1) 1997 Jan:59–82.

The authors adapted the BIARE for use in a self-report questionnaire format.

14. CENSHARE Pet Attachment Scale, PAS (Holcomb, Williams, Richards, 1985)

See CENSHARE Pet Attachment Scale in the measures.

15. Center for the Study of Animal Wellness Pet Bonding Scale, CSAWPBS (Johnson, Meadows, 2003)

See Center for the Study of Animal Wellness Pet Bonding Scale in the measures.

Child Pet Attachment Scale (Melson, 1988)

See Pet Attachment Scale-Revised (Melson 1988) in the measures.

16. Childhood Pet Ownership Questionnaire (Paul, Serpell, 1993)

See Childhood Pet Ownership Questionnaire in the measures.

17. Children and Animals Assessment Instrument, CAAI (Ascione, Thompson, Black, 1997)

Available in:

Clinical assessment of juvenile animal cruelty (Lewchanin, Zimmerman, 2000). See entry in this bibliography.

Reported in:

Ascione, Frank R.; Thompson, Teresa M.; Black, Tracy. Childhood cruelty to animals: Assessing cruelty dimensions and motivations. *Anthrozoös,* 10(4) 1997:170–7.

> This paper is followed by commentaries by Barbara W. Boat and J. S. J. Odendaal, pages 179–80, and by Interviewer Guides Used in Cruelty Research, by Arnold Arluke, pages 180–82. The sample sections given in Appendix A are the CAAI Youth Forms, Perform Cruelty Items for Pet Animals, and Witness Cruelty Items for Pet Animals. There are separate sections about performing or witnessing kindness or cruelty to farm, wild, pet, and stray animals, and parallel youth and parent forms of the CAAI. Appendix B gives rating instructions for the Perform Section of the CAAI in terms of severity, frequency, duration, recency, diversity/across categories, diversity/within category, sentience, covert, isolated, and sentience.

Used in:

Dadds, Mark R.; Whiting, Clare; Bunn, Paul; Fraser, Jennifer A.; Charlson, Juliana H.; Pirola-Merlo, Andrew. Measurement of cruelty in children: The Children and Animals Inventory. *Journal of Abnormal Child Psychology,* 32(3) 2004 Jun:321–34.

> Use the Children's Attitudes and Behaviors toward Animals, CABTA, and Ascione's nine parameters of cruelty to develop the Children and Animals Inventory, CAI.

Guymer, Elise C.; Mellor, David; Luk, Ernest S. L.; Pearse, Vicky. The development of a screening questionnaire for childhood cruelty to animals. *Journal of Child Psychology and Psychiatry,* 42(8) 2001:157–63.

> These authors developed a "shorter, more easily administered [parent-report] questionnaire," the Children's Attitudes and Behaviors toward Animals, CABTA.

Merz-Perez, Linda; Heide, Kathleen M.; Silverman, Ira J. Childhood cruelty to animals and subsequent violence against humans. *International Journal of Offender Therapy and Comparative Criminology,* 45(5) 2001:556–73.

> Use the Survivor's Coping Strategies (SCS) Survey (Heide, Solomon 1991) and the CAAI in face-to-face interviews.

Children and Animals Inventory, CAI

See the entry Cruelty to Animals Inventory, CAI (Dadds et al., 2004).

18. Children's Apperception Test (Animal Figures), CAT(A)

Projective test using ten drawings of animals in various social situations. Prepared as a downward extension of the Thematic Apperception Test (Murray 1943). Designed to aid in understanding a child's relationship to important figures and drives, concerned with feeding problems, sibling rivalry, relations with parents as a couple, etc. The Children's Apperception Test-Supplement, consisting of irregularly shaped pictures in a jigsaw-puzzle format, is available for use in exploration of tension or with children who do not tell stories easily.

> Available from C.P.S., Inc., Box 83, Larchmont, NY 10538-0083.

> Additional information is available from the Educational Testing Service database, at the websites www.ets.org/ and http://sydneyplus.ets.org/.

19. Children's Attitudes and Behaviors toward Animals, CABTA (Guymer et al., 2001)

See Children's Attitudes and Behaviors toward Animals, CABTA, in the measures.

20. Children's Observation and Experience with their Pets, COEP (Ascione, Weber, 1995)

Used in:

Weber, Claudia V. A descriptive study of the relation between domestic violence and pet abuse. 1988. [345] pages. Unpublished Ph.D. thesis, Utah State University, 1998. Adviser: Frank R. Ascione. Abstract in *Dissertation Abstracts International,* Section B: Sciences & Engineering, 59(8-B) 1999 Feb:4492-B.

Also uses the Conflict Tactics Scale, the Battered Partner Shelter Survey, Families and Pets Survey, and the Child Behavior Checklist, CBCL.

21. Children's Representations of Pets (McNicholas, Collis, 2001)

McNicholas, June; Collis, Glyn M. Children's representations of pets in their social networks. *Child: Care, Health and Development,* 27(3) 2001:279–94.

The story-based methodology, which permits seven- to eight-year-old children to nominate their own significant relationships, is given on pages 282–86.

22. Children's Treatment of Animals Questionnaire, CTAQ (Thompson, Gullone, 2003)

See Children's Treatment of Animals Questionnaire, CTAQ, in the measures.

23. Clinical Assessment of Juvenile Animal Cruelty (Lewchanin, Zimmerman, 2000)

Lewchanin, Shari; Zimmerman, Ellen. *Clinical assessment of juvenile animal cruelty.* Brunswick, Maine: Biddle Publishing Company & Audenreed Press, 2000. The Clinical Assessment of Juvenile Animal Cruelty scale addresses overall dynamics and intervention. The parent interview assesses family or caregiver background, which includes violence, and the incidence of childhood cruelty. The child interview assesses background information (school, hobbies), experiences with pets, the incidence of animal abuse, and environmental information (including child abuse, sexual abuse, and family environment).

Includes other scales: Children and Animals Assessment Instrument (CAAI; Ascione et al., 1997); Assessment of Dangerousness in Perpetrators of Animal Cruelty (Lockwood 1988); Juvenile Culpability Assessment (Hindman 1982); a summary sheet and a motivation checklist by Lewchanin; a scale based on the work by Wolin and Wolin (1993) to assess a child's resiliency; a readiness for change scale that incorporates the work of Prochaska, Norcross, and DiClemente (1994); and a scoring sheet and grids taking each into account.

This book is reviewed on pages 379–80 of Duncan, Alex; Miller, Catherine, The impact of an abusive family context on childhood animal cruelty and adult violence, *Aggression and Violent Behavior,* 7(4) 2002 Jul–Aug:265–83.

This book accompanies the authors' *Community intervention in juvenile animal cruelty* (Brunswick, Maine: Biddle Publishing Company & Audenreed Press, 2000.

24. Comfort from Companion Animals Scale, CCAS (Zasloff, 1996)

See the Comfort from Companion Animals Scale, CCAS in the measures.

Commitment to Pets Scale (Staats et al., 1996)

See the Miller-Rada Commitment to Pets Scale (1996) in the measures.

Companion Animal Attachment Scale (McCutcheon, Fleming, 2002)

See the Lexington Attachment to Pets Scale (Johnson, Garrity, Stallones, 1992) in the measures.

25. Companion Animal Bonding Scale, CABS (Poresky et al., 1987)

See the Companion Animal Bonding Scale, CABS in the measures.

Animal Loss Scale (McCutcheon, Fleming, 2002)

See the Lexington Attachment to Pets Scale (Johnson, Garrity, Stallones, 1992) in the measures.

26. Companion Animal Semantic Differential, CAS (Poresky et al., 1988)

See the Companion Animal Semantic Differential, CAS, in the measures.

27. Cruelty to Animals Inventory, CAI (Dadds et al., 2004)

Developed and published in:

Dadds, Mark R.; Whiting, Clare; Bunn, Paul; Fraser, Jennifer A.; Charlson, Juliana H.; Pirola-Merlo, Andrew. Measurement of cruelty in children: The Cruelty to Animals Inventory. *Journal of Abnormal Child Psychology,* 32(3) 2004 Jun:321–34.

> Use the Children and Animals Assessment Inventory, CAAI (Ascione, Thompson, Black 1997) and Children's Attitudes and Behaviors toward Animals (Guymer et al., 2001), which is a parent-report questionnaire, to develop the CAI. Examine reliability and validity of the CAI and whether the self- and parent-reports predict actual behavior. Include the CAI (Appendix A, pages 331–3) and Scoring Chart (pages 333–4). Also use the CAI—P (Children and Animals Inventory—Parent version), "a selection of measures of child adjustment and parenting style . . ." (page 325), and the Children and Animals—Child version (CAI—C). Also use the Alabama Parenting Questionnaire (APQ; Shelton, Frick, Wooton 1996) and the Strengths and Difficulties Questionnaire (SDQ; Goodman 1997). The CAI-C is published in Appendix A, pages 331–3.

28. Demographic and Pet History Questionnaire, DPHQ (Banks, Banks, 2002)

Banks, Marian R.; Banks, William A. The effects of animal-assisted therapy on loneliness in an elderly population in long-term care facilities. *Journals of Gerontology: Medical Sciences,* 57A(7) 2002 Jul:M428-M432.

> Table 1 on page M429 reproduces the DPHQ.
>
> "[A] 26-item instrument . . . used . . . to elicit data on demography, the history of pet ownership, the ages of pet ownership, the types of pets previously owned, the length of ownership, and the desire to have an animal in the long-term care facility. . . . The preference for a particular pet is ascertained by a verbal response" (page M430).
>
> Uses the DPHQ and Version 3 of the UCLA Loneliness Scale (UCLA-LS).

29. Dog Attitude Questionnaire, DAQ (Miura, Bradshaw, Tanida 2000)

Used in:

Miura, Ayaka; Bradshaw, John; Tanida, Hajime. Attitudes towards dogs: A study of university students in Japan and the UK. *Anthrozoös,* 13(2) 2000:80–8.

Miura, Ayaka; Bradshaw, John; Tanida, Hajime. Attitudes towards assistance dogs in Japan and the UK: A comparison of college students studying animal care. *Anthrozoös,* 15(3) 2002:227–42.

This questionnaire was translated into Japanese and back-translated into English to verify its content.

30. Dog Care Responsibility Inventory (Davis, 1987)

See the Dog Care Responsibility Inventory in the measures.

31. Domestic Violence Pet Abuse Survey, DVPAS (Ascione, 2000)

Used by:

Faver, Catherine A; Strand, Elizabeth B. To leave or stay? battered women's concern for vulnerable pets. *Journal of Interpersonal Violence,* 18(12) 2003 Dec:1367–77.

Faver and Strand used only three questions: 1. Has your partner ever threatened to hurt or kill one of your pets? 2. Has your partner ever actually hurt or killed one of your pets? 3. Does concern over your pet's welfare affect your decision making about staying with or leaving your partner? (Cf. page 1372).

32. Equine Client Attachment Checklist (Brackenridge, Shoemaker, 1996)

Brackenridge, Sandra S.; Shoemaker, R. Stuart. The human/horse bond and client bereavement in equine practice, part 1. *Equine Practice,* 18(1) 1996 Jan:19–22.

The checklist is published as Table 1 (page 22).

"Although most veterinarians are automatically aware of an owner's attachment through their observation of affection toward the animal and conversations with the client, many clients are private, stoic, or reserved. An Equine Client Attachment Checklist may be helpful [to veterinarians] in describing the characteristics and behavior of bonded vs. non-bonded clients. In addition, the checklist will identify clients who are very attached and who may need assistance during their bereavement" (page 22).

Twenty-three items are listed. Stronger attachments are reflected by more items checked. If all items are checked, the client is very attached. If only one or two are checked, the client may be only mildly bonded to the horse. The more frequent the contact and the longer the relation between client and the horse, the stronger the bond will be.

33. Human-Animal Relationship Scale (Keil, 1991)

Developed in:

Keil, Carolyn Ivey Pugh. Conceptual framework of human-animal relationships. 1990. [194] pages. Unpublished Ph.D. thesis, University of Kansas, 1990. Abstract in *Dissertation Abstracts International,* Section B: Sciences & Engineering, 52(2-B) 1991 Aug:749-B.

Also uses factors from the Revised Philadelphia Geriatric Center Morale Scale as measures of loneliness and stress, and one-item measures of confounding and demographic variables.

Also used by:

Keil, Carolyn P. Loneliness, stress, and human-animal attachment among older adults, chapter 7, pages 123–34, of *Companion animals in human health,* edited by Cindy C. Wilson and Dennis C. Turner. (Thousand Oaks, CA: Sage Publications, 1998).

34. Human/Pet Relationships Measure (Siegel, 1990)

See the Human/Pet Relationships Measure in the measures.

35. Inventory of Pet Attachment, IPA (Andrews, 1992)

Developed in:

Andrews, Sandra Lee. The Inventory of Pet Attachment: Development and validation. 1992. iv, 94 leaves. Unpublished Ph.D. thesis, Texas A&M University, 1992. Not seen. Abstract in *Dissertation Abstracts International,* Section B: Sciences & Engineering, 53(9-B) 1993 Mar:4941-B.

> Correlates the Inventory of Pet Attachment, a scale designed to measure nonconventional attachment to pets, with the Pet Attitude Scale (PAS; Templer et al., 1981) and Companion Animal Bonding Scale (CABS; Poresky et al., 1987).

36. Lexington Attachment to Pets Scale, LAPS (Johnson, Garrity, Stallones, 1992)

See the Lexington Attachment to Pets Scale, LAPS in the measures.

Love of Animals and Love of People (Ray 1982)

See the entry Attitude toward Animals and Attitude toward People Scales (Ray 1982).

37. Measurement of Pet Intervention, MOPI (Schiro-Geist, 2001)

See the Measurement of Pet Intervention, MOPI in the measures.

Melson Parent Questionnaire (1988)

See the Pet Attachment Scale—Revised (Melson 1988) in the measures.

38. Miller-Rada Commitment to Pets Scale (Staats et al., 1996)

See the Miller-Rada Commitment to Pets Scale in the measures.

39. Monash Dog Owner Relationship Scale, MDORS (Dwyer, 2003)

Developed in:

Dwyer, Fleur. The creation of a multi-dimensional human-companion animal bonding scale. 2003. Unpublished D.Psy. thesis, University of Monash, 2003. Adviser: Pauleen Bennett.

> Dwyer developed a multidimensional scale that could be used to assess relationships between owners and their companion dogs. The items in the scale were based on appropriate theoretical frameworks including Exchange Theory, Social Support Theory, Quality of Life, and Bonding, as well as aspects of human-companion dog relationships that were identified by owners as important. This scale was developed using sound methodology and stringent statistical techniques. The Monash Dog Owner Relationship Scale (MDORS) has

28 items, which reflect three sub-scales, 1) Dog-Owner Interaction, 2) Emotional Closeness, and 3) Perceived Costs of Companion Dog Ownership. The sub-scales are consistent with theoretical predictions, previously developed scales, and previous research in the human-companion animal relationships field. The MDORS has adequate reliability and established discriminant and convergent validity. The MDORS is the first scale to attempt to assess human relationships with an individual species of companion animal. The results of this study show that assessing human relationships with individual species of companion animals is useful, as many of the important items in the MDORS would not be applicable to other species of companion animal. The MDORS is also the first scale in the area of human-companion animal relationships that extensively addresses the costs associated with companion dog ownership.

Taken from the Monash University Department of Psychology website, www.med.monash.edu.au/psych/ research/carg/staff/fd.html (accessed 10 June 2004).

40. "My Pet" Inventory (Furman, 1989)

Used in:

Furman, Wyndol. The development of children's social networks (chapter 6), pages 151–72 in: Belle, Deborah (editor), *Children's social networks and social supports.* New York: J. Wiley & Sons, 1989.

In one paragraph on pages 167–8 children's relationships with their pets are examined, but they are not included in Table 6.2, page 159.

Published in:

Bryant, Brenda K. The richness of the child-pet relationship: A consideration of both benefits and costs of pets to children. *Anthrozoös,* 3(4) 1990 Spring:253–61.

The factors—mutuality (reciprocity in the caring and loving between pet and child); enduring affection (even if the child misbehaves the pet will still love her); self-enhancing affection (the child-pet relationship is perceived by children as one that makes them feel good about themselves and instills a sense of importance); and exclusivity of child-pet relationship (children value the privacy and confidentiality pets provide in keeping secrets)—and item wording appear in Table 2, page 256.

41. People's Experiences Following the Death of a Pet (Adams, 1996)

See People's Experiences Following the Death of a Pet in the measures.

42. Pet Abuse Potential Scale (Raupp, 1999)

Published in:

Raupp, Carol D. Treasuring, trashing or terrorizing: Adult outcomes of childhood socialization about companion animals. *Society & Animals,* 7(2) 1999:141–59.

Adapted Milner's Child Abuse Potential Scale (1994) by rewording 19 items about children to refer to pets. Also used "a 27-item attachment scale adapted and expanded from a variety of existing measures to capture not only affection but also selective preference . . ." (page 148).

43. Pet and Personal History (Bustad, 1980)

Bustad, Leo K. *Animals, aging, and the aged.* (The Wesley W. Spink lectures on comparative medicine, vol. 5). Minneapolis: University of Minnesota Press, 1980.

This "interviewing guide for pet placement with individuals" appears in chapter 4, The Contributions of

Companion Animals to Human Well Being, pages 137–40. The "interviewing guide for pet placement with an institution" appears on pages 140–43. Table 9, "Human Personality Profile," with instructions for completion by the prospective owner or by a "social worker or other trained person in situations where a pet may be used in therapy," appears on pages 144–45. Canine selection procedures (pages 148–57) and feline selection procedures (pages157–61) follow.

According to the text, all these were to be reviewed and refined by the People-Pet Partnership Program at the Washington State University College of Veterinary Medicine, P. O. Box 64710, Pullman, WA 99164-7010; phone 509/335-1303; fax 509/335-6094.

Pet Attachment Scale, PAS

See the Lexington Attachment to Pets Scale, LAPS (Johnson, Garrity, Stallones 1992) in the measures.

44. Pet Attachment Scale, PAS (Chumley et al., 1993)

Developed for:

Chumley, Perry R.; Gorski, June D.; Saxton, Arnold M.; Granger, Ben P.; New, John C., Jr. Companion animal attachment and military transfer. *Anthrozoös*, 6(4) 1993:258–73.

This is a combination of the Pet Relationship Scales 1 and 2 (Kafer et al., 1992) and seven items from the Pet Attitude Scale (Templer et al., 1981), to form a 21-item Pet Attachment Scale with a six-point Likert scale. It appears on pages 272–73.

45. Pet Attachment Scale, PAS (Geller, 2005)

Developed in:

Geller, Christa Scott. Quantifying the power of pets: The development of an assessment device to measure attachment between humans and companion animals. 2005. Unpublished Ph.D. thesis, Human Development, Virginia Technical Institute & State University, 2005. Chair, Advisory Committee: Fred P. Piercy. Not seen. Abstract available at the website http://scholar.lib.vet.edu/theses/available/etd-04252005-171588/ (accessed 10 Oct 2005).

Develops and evaluates a 34-item Pet-Attachment Scale, PAS and compares it with the Companion Animal Bonding Scale, CABS (Poresky et al., 1987).The factor analysis of the PAS reveals two factors: Companionship (12 items) and Emotional fulfillment (7 items). Thus the PAS could be shortened to 19 items for follow-up research. The factor analysis for CABS reveals one factor (caretaking) and the analysis suggests it could be reduced from 8 to 3 items. The strong correlations between the PAS and CABS suggest concurrent, convergent, and construct validity for the PAS.

46. Pet Attachment Scale – Revised (Melson, 1988)

See the Pet Attachment Scale—Revised in the measures.

47. Pet Attachment Scale – Parent Report (Melson, 1988)

See the Pet Attachment Scale—Revised (Melson 1988) in the measures.

48. Pet Attachment Worksheet, PAW (Greene, Landis, 2002)

49. Pet Attachment Worksheet for Children (Greene, Landis, 2002)

Greene, Lorri A.; Landis, Jacquelyn. Saying goodbye to the pet you love: A complete resource to help you heal. Oakland, Calif.: New Harbinger Publications, 2002.

The Pet Attachment Worksheet is a self-administered, 7-point Likert scale, presented on pages 18–20.

The Pet Attachment Worksheet for Children on pages 122–3 is intended for parents in discussing pet loss and its effects with their children.

50. Pet Attitude Inventory, PAI (Wilson, Netting, New, 1987)

See the Pet Attitude Inventory, PAI, in the measures.

51. Pet Attitude Scale—Modified, PAS-M (Templer et al., 1981)

See the Pet Attitude Scale—Modified, PAS-M, in the measures.

Pet Bonding Scale (Johnson, Meadows, 2003)

See the Center for the Study of Animal Wellness Pet Bonding Scale, CSAWPBS, in the measures.

52. Pet Bonding Scale, PBS (Angle, Blumentritt, Swank, 1993)

See the Pet Bonding Scale, PBS, in the measures.

53. Pet Care Experience and Pet Attachment Scale (Robertson, Gallivan, MacIntyre, 2004)

Published in:

Robertson, Jessie C; Gallivan, Joanne; MacIntyre, Peter D. Sex differences in the antecedents of animal use attitudes. *Anthrozoös,* 17(4) 2004:306–39.

Appendix 2. Eighteen-item scale used to measure pet care experience and pet attachment. 1 = never, 2 = seldom, 3 = occasionally, 4 = frequently, 5 = always. Items 1 and 2 are yes/no, but 1b and 2b are rated on the five point scale. Intended to measure both pet care experience and pet attachment. Some of the statements in the scale were taken from the Pet Attitude Inventory (Wilson, Netting, New 1988) and others were developed for this study.

54. Pet Costs Inventory (Bryant, 1990)

Published in:

Bryant, Brenda K. The richness of the child-pet relationship: A consideration of both benefits and costs of pets to children. *Anthrozoös,* 3(4) 1990 Spring:253–61.

The factors and item wording appear in table 4, page 258.

55. Pet Expectations Inventory, PEI (George, 1992)

See the Pet Expectations Inventory, PEI, in the measures.

56. Pet/Friend Q-Sort, PFQ (Davis, 1986)

The PFQ consists of 60 positive affective statements. It is an earlier version of the Pet Friendship Scale, which is reproduced in the measures.

It is developed and included in Janet Haggerty Davis's Ph.D. thesis, The role of the family dog in the preadolescent's psychosocial development relative to selected dimensions of the self-concept, sex, and age (Loyola University, Chicago, 1986).

It is used in her article, Preadolescent self-concept development and pet ownership, *Anthrozoös,* 8(2) 1995:78–82.

57. Pet Friendship Scale, PFS (Davis, 1995)

See the Pet Friendship Scale, PFS in the measures.

58. Pet Loss and Religious Issues Interview (Davis et al., 2003)

Reported in:

Davis, Helen; Irwin, Peter; Richardson, Michelle; O'Brien-Malone, Angela. When a pet dies: Religious issues, euthanasia and strategies for coping with bereavement. *Anthrozoös,* 16(1) 2003:57–74.

> This title does not appear in this citation and was assigned by the editor. Table 2, "Key questions and prompts in the semi-structured interview," on page 64 presents the questions used in the interview.

59. Pet Loss Questionnaire (Planchon et al., 2002)

Used and reported in:

Planchon, Lynn A.; Templer, Donald I.; Stokes, Shelley; Keller, Jacqueline. Death of a companion cat or dog and human bereavement: Psychosocial variables. *Society & Animals,* 10(1) 2002:93–105.

> Use the Beck Depression Inventory, BDI (Beck et al., 1961), the CENSHARE Pet Attachment Survey (Holcomb, Williams and Richards, 1985), the Pet Attitude Scale (Templer et al., 1981), and the Pet Loss Questionnaire. The Pet Loss Questionnaire appears in table 1, pages 96–97, and is also available at the website, www.societyandanimalsform.org/sa/sa10.1/planchon.shtml (accessed August 10, 2004). It contains subject demographics, pet loss information, and grief symptoms.

60. Pet Ownership Interview Guide (Allen, Kellegrew, Jaffe, 2000)

Used in:

Allen, Jessica M.; Kellegrew, Diane Harmon; Jaffe, Deborah. The experience of pet ownership as a meaningful occupation. *Canadian Journal of Occupational Therapy = Revue Canadienne d'Ergotherapie,* 67(4) 2000 Oct:271–8.

> Table 1, "Open-ended Interview Guide," page 274, list the ten questions used in The Pet Ownership Interview Guide. The title, Pet Ownership Interview Guide, does not appear in this article, but was assigned by the Health and Psychosocial Instruments (HaPI) staff. The guide is designed to gather information about the experience of pet ownership. Issues to address are set for the respondent before interviewing begins. Then, "open-ended probes are used to clarify and expand upon responses . . . A sample . . . of interview probes used for each of . . . three key issues [follows]" (page 274): Routes (e.g., "On a typical day, what interactions do you have with your pet?"), (b) Affective Domain (e.g., "What feelings do you associate with your pet?"), and (c) Physical Health Domain (e.g., "How does having a pet affect your level of activity?").

61. Pet Ownership Observations (Allen, Kellegrew, Jaffe, 2000)

Used in:

Allen, J. M.; Kellegrew, D. H.; Jaffe, D. The experience of pet ownership as a meaningful occupation. *Canadian Journal of Occupational Therapy = Revue Canadienne d'Ergotherapie,* 67(4) 2000 Oct:271–8.

> The title, Pet Ownership Observations, does not appear in this citation and was assigned by the HaPI staff, consists of "field observations of naturally occurring interactions between . . . participants and their pets. . . . The field observations provide additional information regarding how the pet owner's environment is structured to incorporate their pet. . . . Field notes are written during and after the observations" (page 274).

62. Pet Personality Trait Rating Scale (Gosling, Bonnenburg, 1998)

Published in:

Gosling, Samuel D; Bonnenburg, Allison V. An integrative approach to personality research in anthrozoology: Ratings of six species of pets and their owners. *Anthrozoös,* (3) 1998:148–56.

> The title, Pet Personality Trait Rating Scale, does not appear in this citation and was assigned by the editor. It appears as Appendix A, "How accurately do these traits describe your pet?" (see page 156).

63. Pet Relationship Impact Inventory (Eckstein, 2000)

Developed in:

Eckstein, Daniel. The Pet Relationship Impact Inventory. *Family Journal: Counseling & Therapy for Couples & Families,* 8(2) 2000 Apr:192–8.

> This inventory, which is for self-administration and for use with one's own family, appears on page 193. The article and inventory also appear on the author's website at: www.encouragingleadership.com/pet_relationship.htm (accessed 10 July 2002).

Used by:

Shore, Elsie R.; Petersen, Connie L.; Douglas, Deanne K. Moving as a reason for pet relinquishment: A closer look. *Journal of Applied Animal Welfare Science,* 6(1) 2003:39–52.

> Uses a human-animal bonding scale, based on the Companion Animal Bonding Scale (Poresky et al., 1987) and the Pet Relationship Impact Inventory.

64. Pet Relationship Scales, PRS (Kafer et al., 1992)

See the Pet Relationship Scales, PRS, in the measures.

65. Pet Visitation Program Survey Form (Fried, 1996)

Developed in:

Fried, Karen P. Pet-facilitated therapy as adjunctive care for home hospice patients: A human service program design to promote quality of life. 1996. [78] pages. Unpublished Psy.D. thesis, Rutgers, The State University of New Jersey, Graduate Applied and Professional Psychology, 1996. Not seen. Abstract in *Dissertation Abstracts International,* Section B: Sciences & Engineering, 57(5-B) 1996 Nov:3409-B.

66. Physical and Emotional Tormenting against Animals Scale, P.E.T. (Baldry, 2004)

Developed in:

Baldry, Anna C. The development of the P.E.T. Scale for the measurement of physical and emotional tormenting against animals in adolescents. *Society & Animals,* 12(1) 2004:1–17.

    The P.E.T. scale is reproduced in the appendix, pages 13–14.

67. Quality of Life Offered by Bird Ownership (Anderson, 2001)

Used in:

Anderson, Patricia K. Our feathered friends: Avian companions in everyday life. 2001. Paper invited for presentation at the symposium Human/Animal Interaction in Everyday Life, Midwest Sociology Meetings, April 5–8, 2001.

Anderson, Patricia K. A bird in the house: An anthropological perspective on companion parrots. *Society & Animals,* 11(4) 2003:393–418.

68. Relinquishment Questionnaire (Mondelli et al., 2004)

Used in:

Mondelli, Francesca; Prato Previde, Emanuela; Verga, Marina; Levi, Diana; Magistrelli, Sonia; Valsecchi, Paola. The bond that never developed: Adoption and relinquishment of dogs in a rescue shelter. *Journal of Applied Animal Welfare Science,* 7(4) 2004:253–66.

    The Relinquishment Questionnaire is reproduced on pages 265–66.

69. Service Animal Adaptive Intervention Assessment, SAAIA (Zapf, Rough, 2002)

Developed in:

Zapf, S.A.; Rough, R.B. The development of an instrument to match individuals with disabilities and service animals. *Disability & Rehabilitation: An International Multidisciplinary Journal,* 24(1–3), 2002 Jan:47–58.

    The authors developed the SAAIA and measured its content validity, inter-rater reliability and clinical utility. Results, using a group of occupational therapists and physical therapists and another group of health care professionals with experience or background in animal assisted therapy or service animals, show that content validity indicated a good to high percentage of agreement and clinical utility, a fair percentage of agreement. Inter-rater reliability results indicate a good to high agreement on six of the eight variables. The Kappa score indicates low inter-rater reliability. The authors conclude that the SAAIA has good content validity and inter-rater reliability and fair clinical utility based on percentage agreement.

Survey for Military Animal Owners

See the Pet Attachment Scale, PAS (Chumley et al., 1993) in the measures.

70. Survey on Pet Animals in the Classroom (Rud, Beck, 2003)

Used in:

Rud, Anthony G., Jr.; Beck, Alan M. Companion animals in Indiana elementary schools. *Anthrozoös,* 16(3) 2003:241–51.

    A descriptive study from a convenience sample of rural, suburban and urban teachers in Indiana.
    "The Survey on Pet Animals in the Classroom—1998," is reproduced as appendix I, page 251.

71. Le Travail en élevage [Work with Livestock] (Porcher, Cousson-Gelie, Dantzer, 2004)

Used in:

Porcher, Jocelyne; Cousson-Gelie, Florence; Dantzer, Robert. Affective components of the human-animal relationship in animal husbandry: Development and validation of a questionnaire. *Psychological Reports,* 95(1) 2004 Aug:275–90.

Five items (5, 6, 8, 10, and 22) of this survey of 26 items were removed from the analysis and not presented in the text. The remaining 21 items are listed in English in Table 2 (page 281) and throughout the text. These 21 items require back-translation into French to verify the English translation.

The order of the Likert scale given on page 21 is 1= Disagree quite a lot, 2 = Disagree, 3 = Don't know, 4 = Agree quite a lot; 5 = Agree. The text says, "'Don't know' represent[s] an intermediate value."

However, the order of the Likert scale in the questionnaire is: 1 = Strongly disagree, 2 = Disagree, 3 = Agree, 4 = Strongly agree; 5 = Don't know.

Name Index of Authors of the Measures Cited

This index is arranged A–Z by authors of the contributions cited in the Index & Bibliography. The item numbers are those listed in the Index & Bibliography. This will permit you to go from any one of the authors of a measure to the Index & Bibliography for citations to the individual measures.

For example, if you know that John Rhoades participated in preparation or validation of a measure, you will find under his name, item 10, Attitudes toward Responsible Pet Ownership, which is fully cited in the Index & Bibliography.

Adams, Cindy L.	41	People's Experiences Following the Death of a Pet
Allen, Jessica M.	60	Pet Ownership Interview Guide
	61	Pet Ownership Observations
Anderson, Patricia K.	67	Quality of Life Offered by Bird Ownership.
Andrews, Sandra Lee	35	Inventory of Pet Attachment, IPA
Angle, Rebecca L.	52	Pet Bonding Scale, PBS
Arikawa, Hiroko	51	Pet Attitude Scale—Modified, PAS-M
Ascione, Frank R.	11	Battered Partner Shelter, Survey, BPSS/Pet Maltreatment Survey
	12	Battered Partner Shelter Survey, BPSS/Pet Maltreatment Survey. Mother/Child Version
	17	Children and Animals Assessment Instrument, CAAI
	20	Children's Observation and Experience with their Pets, COEP
	31	Domestic Violence Pet Abuse Survey, DVPAS
Baker, Dewleen G.	13	Boat Inventory on Animal-Related Experiences, BIARE
Baldry, Anna C.	66	Physical and Emotional Tormenting against Animals Scale, P.E.T.
Baldwin, Roy	51	Pet Attitude Scale—Modified, PAS-M
Banks, Marian R.	28	Demographic and Pet History Questionnaire, DPHQ
Banks, William A.	28	Demographic and Pet History Questionnaire, DPHQ
Beck, Alan M.	70	Survey on Pet Animals in the Classroom
Bennett, Pauleen	39	Monash Dog Owner Relationship Scale, MDORS
Black, Tracy	17	Children and Animals Assessment Instrument, CAAI
Blumentritt, Tracie L.	52	Pet Bonding Scale, PBS
Boat, Barbara W.	13	Boat Inventory on Animal-Related Experiences, BIARE

Appendix

Aline H. Kidd and Robert M. Kidd Publications on People and Pets

Kidd, Aline H.; Kidd, Robert M. Personality characteristics and preferences in pet ownership. *Psychological Reports,* 46(3, pt1) 1980 Jun:939–49.

Martinez, Robin L.; Kidd, Aline H. Two personality characteristics in adult pet-owners and non-owners. *Psychological Reports,* 47(1) 1980 Aug:318.

Kidd, Aline H.; Feldmann, Bruce Max. Pet ownership and self-perceptions of older people. *Psychological Reports,* 48(3) 1981 Jun:867–75.

Kidd, Aline H.; Kelley, Helen T.; Kidd, Robert M. Personality characteristics of horse, turtle, snake, and bird owners. *Psychological Reports,* 52(3) 1983 Jun:719–29.

Kidd, Aline H.; Kelley, Helen T.; Kidd, Robert M. Personality characteristics of horse, turtle, snake, and bird owners, pages 200–6, in: The Pet Connection: Proceedings of the Minnesota-California Conferences on the Human-Animal Bond, Robert K. Anderson, Benjamin L. Hart, Lynette A. Hart, editors. Minneapolis: Center to Study Human-Animal Relationships, University of Minnesota, 1984.

Kidd, Aline H.; Kidd, Robert M. Children's attitudes toward their pets. *Psychological Reports,* 57(1) 1985 Aug:15–31.

Kidd, Aline H.; Kidd, Robert M. Reactions of infants and toddlers to live and toy animals. *Psychological Reports,* 61(2) 1987 Oct:455–64.

Kidd, Aline H.; Kidd, Robert M. Seeking a theory of the human/companion animal bond. *Anthrozoös,* 1(3) 1987 Winter:140–5.

Kidd, A. H.; Kidd, R. M. Factors in adults' attitudes toward pets. *Psychological Reports,* 65(3, pt1) 1989 Dec:903–10.

Kidd, A. H.; Kidd, R. M. Factors in children's attitudes toward pets. *Psychological Reports,* 66(3, pt1) 1990 Jun:775–86.

Kidd, R. M.; Kidd, A. H. High school students and their pets. *Psychological Reports,* 66(3, pt 2) 1990 Jun:1391–4.

Kidd, Aline H.; Kidd, Robert M. Social and environmental influences on children's attitudes toward pets. *Psychological Reports,* 67(3, pt 1) 1990 Dec:807–18.

Kidd, Aline H.; Kidd, Robert M.; George, Carol C. Successful and unsuccessful pet adoptions. *Psychological Reports,* 70(2) 1992 Apr:547–61.

Kidd, Aline H.; Kidd, Robert M.; George, Carol C. Veterinarians and successful pet adoptions. *Psychological Reports,* 71(2) 1992 Oct:551–7.

Kidd, Aline H.; Kidd, Robert M. Benefits and liabilities of pets for the homeless. *Psychological Reports,* 74(3, pt1) 1994 Jun:715–22.

Zasloff, Ruth L.; Kidd, Aline H. Attachment to feline companions. *Psychological Reports,* 74(3, pt1) 1994 Jun:747–52.

Zasloff, R. Lee; Kidd, Aline H. Loneliness and pet ownership among single women. *Psychological Reports,* 75(2) 1994 Oct:747–52.

Kidd, Aline H.; Kidd, Robert M.; Zasloff, R. Lee. Developmental factors in positive attitudes toward zoo animals. *Psychological Reports,* 76(1) 1995 Feb:71–81.

Kidd, Aline H.; Kidd, Robert M. Children's drawings and attachment to pets. *Psychological Reports,* 77(1) 1995 Aug:235–41.

Kidd, Aline H.; Kidd, Robert M. Developmental factors leading to positive attitudes toward wildlife and conservation. *Applied Animal Behaviour Science,* 47(1–2) 1996 Apr:119–25.

Kidd, Aline H.; Kidd, Robert M.; Zasloff, R. Lee. Characteristics and motives of volunteers in wildlife rehabilitation. *Psychological Reports,* 79(1) 1996 Aug:227–34.

Kidd, Aline H.; Kidd, Robert M. Changes in the behavior of pet owners across generations. *Psychological Reports,* 80(1) 1997 Feb:195–202.

Kidd, Aline H.; Kidd, Robert M. Characteristics and motives of adolescent volunteers in wildlife education. *Psychological Reports,* 80(3, pt1) 1997 Jun:747–53.

Kidd, Aline H.; Kidd, Robert M. Characteristics and motives of docents in wildlife education. *Psychological Reports,* 81(2) 1997 Oct:383–6.

Kidd, Aline H.; Kidd, Robert M. Problems and benefits of bird ownership. *Psychological Reports,* 83(1) 1998 Aug:131–8.

Kidd, Aline H.; Kidd, Robert M. Addendum to Problems and benefits of bird ownership. *Psychological Reports,* 84(2) 1999 Apr:368–70.

Kidd, Aline H.; Kidd, Robert M. Benefits, problems, and characteristics of home aquarium owners. *Psychological Reports,* 84(3, pt 1) 1999 Jun:998–1004.

Printed in the USA
CPSIA information can be obtained
at www.ICGtesting.com
LVHW020844060823
754382LV00018B/270